YOU MAKE THE DIFFERENCE

THROUGH

INSPIRING COMMUNITY SUSTAINABILITY

Kay Kay

In collaboration with Tim Kay

You Make the Difference
www.youmakethedifference.net

First Edition
Published 2013

Book designed and published by Tim Kay
University of Life

www.unioflife.net

You Make the Difference logo © Tim Kay
All other illustrations and images © Microsoft Corporation

Author photo by Lina&Linda AB
Stockholm, Sweden

DEDICATION

This book is dedicated to the people who
make a positive difference in their communities.

CONTENTS

ACKNOWLEDGMENTS

While initiating or supporting, consulting or coaching, volunteering or benefiting from so many groups and projects, it has been my privilege to meet some extraordinarily dedicated people making a huge difference in their communities.

I am especially appreciative of my colleagues and friends in the Findhorn Community whose work on sustainability is outstanding; to Sir John Whitmore, whose insights into the three stages of team development in his book, Coaching for Performance, has informed and inspired my work on the stages of community development; to the fine people who contribute to the Transition Town Network, to the website for Living Communities, the one for CoHousing and Wikipedia for the information on Sociocracy; to Lawrence Demarco and the team at Social Enterprise Scotland for their interesting and useful information.

I have included some extracts from other people's writing and from websites that succinctly describe the topic being explored. The sources are within the text. I appreciate the work, insights and dedication of those writers and I encourage the further reading of their material.

Most of my writing is based upon decades of experience and on the results of my search around the Globe seeking information and wisdom. As this was mostly for my own development it became embodied rather than recorded in writing. As processes are frequently adopted and adapted by trainers, workshop leaders and facilitators, it can become impossible to trace the originators. Consequently, the sources of much of what I now know are lost in the mists of time and I am unable to acknowledge the originators of some of the information in this book. So I am able only to offer my general appreciation to all those whose work has paved the way for the current understanding of what can ensure the sustainability of our communities.

KAY KAY

1

WHAT IS COMMUNITY SUSTAINABILITY?

In order to explore methods for inspiring community sustainability it could be useful to first consider what community sustainability means.

Q

What do we mean by 'sustainability'?

Despite being a fashionable word that features prominently in the media, in politics, in economic and environmental predictions and in many people's conversations, there seems to be no simple, clearly agreed-upon practical definition of sustainability.

Some people might describe sustainability as survival strategies for species or ecological and economical systems. Others would define it through social factors: human beings' relationship to nature, spirituality, wisdom, personal and community development, equality, holistic decision-making processes, living consciously, right livelihood, a commitment to continuance and a sense of place. Dependent upon people's values, the importance placed upon sustainability could be environmental, economical, social or spiritual.

For some people sustainability could mean surviving; for others it would mean thriving, and for others it might mean the process of moving from surviving to thriving in a responsible manner.

For the purposes of this book, sustainability will be taken to mean the following:

The intention to maintain a satisfying, balanced way of life where planet and people matter and are respected.

a) Creating responsible ways of living in, working in and maintaining a sense of community that can be continued into the indefinite future.

b) Maintaining the effective continuance of an intentional community or a community initiative or project.

c) The reasonable use of all resources being equitable to their wisely achievable, renewable and continuous availability.

d) Looking ahead for at least seven generations.

What do we mean by community?

Dictionaries give the definition of community as: a group of people; a neighborhood; or kinship. Under this heading of kinship come the words: unity, identity, cooperation, cooperative spirit, convergence and similarity.

> The urge to gather together in some form of community is fundamental to being human.

This is what has allowed us to evolve into societies that function reasonably well for most citizens around the world. However, in many places, increasingly over the past half-century, there seems to have developed a culture of individuality in which ever greater numbers of people have pursued their desires and goals alone, sometimes without much thought to how the outcomes might impact others.

> Many people are now realizing that this approach to life is not nurturing for the individual and often has a damaging impact upon the planet and upon other people. The numerous benefits of being involved in community in some form are becoming widely recognized.

What Type of Community?

For the purposes of this book communities are described as either being Intentional or Local.

Local communities

Although there are still traditional local communities around the world that are comprised of a single ethnic group and/or where the members follow the same beliefs and agree (more or less) to the same values, most communities these days are made up of people from a variety of backgrounds, with differing religious and political beliefs and outlooks on life. The suggestions in this book are offered to support the sustainability of local communities, especially those with the intention of developing or improving neighborhood cooperation and mutual support; Transition Towns; local area initiatives for improving services and systems and the development of a greater sense community within urban or rural locations.

In most human settlements of villages, towns and cities, some type of community infrastructure already exists, and, in many places, has done so for thousands of years. In such locations there will already be a structure of governance: fully democratic, semi democratic, tribal, feudal or autocratic. Some of these will be supportive of cooperative living and sustainability for all and some may not. In the places in the world where some form of democracy exists, most community improvement initiatives are likely to receive some encouragement and perhaps a degree of financial and other forms of support from local and national government.

For those of us who have this privilege, it is important to remember that this is not the case everywhere around the Globe. There are many places that are still tribal or feudal or where autocracy is based upon a political or religious ideology where engagement in local community decision-making may be limited to a few privileged people. There are dictatorships sustained by military strength and situations where the hierarchy of power is generated by land ownership, extreme wealth of a few individuals or the power over people sustained by fear of violence, incarceration or poverty. There are also areas in this world where no workable governance structure exists; where it has collapsed or is in the process of doing so.

Attempting to improve the infrastructure of communities, initiating systems for mutual support, cooperation and collective decision-making at the grassroots level and endeavoring to have some power devolved from a few to the many, can be hard work, time consuming, difficult and in some places hazardous or extremely dangerous. Even so, there is a global groundswell of interest in the improvement of local communities by people engaging in grassroots initiatives, local projects and community-led regeneration of villagers, towns and city districts.

Much of this grassroots groundswell is resulting in community-led regeneration of towns, villages and inner city areas.

What is community-led regeneration?

The following description is from a 2004 Scottish report on the subject:

Community-led regeneration means that the emphasis in the shape and *direction of the regeneration process shifts from being determined principally by external stakeholders (local government, public agencies) to being determined principally by internal stakeholders (local people). Regeneration strategies in the past have typically incorporated some degree of community involvement with the aim of providing local people with an opportunity to feed into the process and to have their voices heard. Essentially, the role of the community in previous regeneration strategies has been consultative and passive. Community-led regeneration demands a much more proactive contribution from the local community and as such it is not necessarily an approach that will suit all communities.*

Community-led regeneration can take many different forms and these will be determined by local context. However, where community-led regeneration occurs a number of features are likely to be observable in each instance:

1. *One or more local organizations playing the role, or with the potential to play the role, of a community anchor (providing a degree of local leadership and offering support to less formal types of community activity).*
2. *Significant assets under community ownership or control.*
3. *Community owned enterprises generating an income stream.*
4. *A locally conceived community plan or 'charter', which identifies the short, medium and long-term priorities for action as determined by local people.*
5. *A level of engagement with external stakeholders, which reflects a sense of genuine partnership and mutual respect.*
6. *An absence of top down, unilateral public sector-driven initiatives.*

Community-led regeneration requires significant culture change on all sides. Communities need to realize that the public sector is no longer in a position to meet all of their needs or to 'resolve' many of the problems that they face. Public sector agencies need to realize it is neither appropriate nor realistic for them to imagine they should seek to be doing this. In essence, community-led regeneration requires the relationship between the state and communities to be recalibrated so that there is a much greater sense of mutual respect and equality of status

Examples of community-led regeneration can be found in many different places, from the island based community buy outs where local people have assumed control over virtually every aspect of community life, to more urban communities where various combinations of development trusts and community based housing associations have acquired control and ownership over a wide range of assets and enterprises and where local people are now instrumental in shaping their own futures.

Widening the responsibility

It's clear that decisions made by a relatively few powerful or influential people - altruistic or self-interested – often do not properly address the needs and concerns of the majority of people struggling to make their lives and their communities work in the face of social, environmental and economic dysfunction.

> It makes far more sense for the people who are most effected to have a say in what is needed, to have a voice in the decision-making and a hand in the required actions.

Many people are no longer prepared to put up with social situations that do not serve them well. They are increasingly dissatisfied with the decisions that affect their lives that are made by others who have not taken their concerns, needs and views into consideration.

The cultural and social changes being experienced in many places around the world have created the necessity for increased community engagement. This has provided opportunities for people to recreate their communities in the way of their own choosing.

Many community groups and projects are now contributing to one of the most significant social changes to take place in recent times. This is the ever-increasing numbers of citizens becoming proactively involved in projects to improve their local communities in villages, towns and city districts.

People are no longer feeling powerless to influence the future of the areas in which they live. They are getting together, in groups large or small, to bring about the changes they desire to see in their communities. More and more people are willing to become involved in community projects and are stepping up to take some responsibility for making beneficial things happen.

This is rarely done in isolation. Just at the time when it is important for people to become engaged in creating the future they wish to see, there are systems available which can help:

a) Ready-made mechanisms for sharing information and offering mutual support.

b) Many individuals, groups and organizations with expertise and experience in community processes that can assist.

c) Networks, local, national and global, through which useful information can be shared.

What are Transition Towns?

Much of this Community-led regeneration is taking place within the Transition Towns movement, which was started in Totness in Southern England, and has now reached global proportions. This movement offers a great deal of valuable information and tried and trusted formulas and models for community regeneration and particularly for increased local environmental sustainability. Visit: http://www.transitionnetwork.org.

The regeneration of a community requires involvement, input, discussion and decision-making by as wide a range of the community's citizens as possible. Community groups and organizations that have been and continue to be formed for specific purposes can carry out many, and in some cases, most of the necessary activities, services and projects within a community. Sensible community groups will have an awareness of what other community groups are doing and will have the intention of being mutually supportive to one another.

Intentional communities

These are created by people who consciously choose to live and, usually, although not always, work together.

Intentional Community is an inclusive term for intentional living, alternative communities, cooperative living, Ecovillages, Cohousing communities, residential land trusts, communes, student co-ops, urban housing cooperatives and other projects where people strive together with a common vision.

Some communities seem to form themselves as people gather naturally around a common interest, a mutual need or an inspiring idea. On some occasions the idea for a community comes first that is created to achieve some purpose and to which people turn up to join. At other times a nucleus of people who want to live and/or work together initiate a community through which they can do so.

What is Cohousing?

The Fellowship of Intentional Communities gives the following description of CoHousing:

Though there is no precise definition, cohousing communities have characteristics that they typically share. The widely quoted Six Defining Characteristics of Cohousing is published in full on the Coho/US website.

While cohousing communities may appear similar to some mainstream housing developments, the people forming cohousing communities organize to practice ideals of participation, cooperation, sharing, and knowing one's neighbors. Cohousing communities, typically, use private, home ownership as part of the community's economic model - making it relatively easy for forming groups to obtain construction and mortgage financing from conventional banks.

The vast majority of existing cohousing communities had considerable resident input into the design process as it unfolds. For neighborhood-level cohousing, Site designs generally cluster housing with enhanced pedestrian and play areas to promote frequent, spontaneous human contact - cars (roads and parking) are usually de-emphasized and set apart from the homes and primary common spaces. Cohousing can also take other forms, including large, shared buildings, and groups of existing dwellings that are retrofitted into Cohousing communities. While many, and probably most, cohousing communities have been self-developed, there are an increasing number of cohousing projects that start with leadership from commercial developers.

Most cohousing communities have a "common house", a building (or space within a larger building) that most often includes a large kitchen and dining room, with a wide range of other possible facilities. This shared space is intended to act as an extension of the individual private homes, and many cohousing homes are smaller than their non-community counterparts.

Most cohousing communities operate using Consensus decision-making. While there is no typical "Cohousing system" for governance, there is emerging interest in Sociocracy models. (Covered later in chapters on Governance and Decision-making).

Q

What is an intentional community?

The following description of some aspects of Intentional Community living is based upon the article: What's True About Intentional Communities, compiled by the Fellowship for Intentional Communities, October 1996. Although the number of intentional communities has grown enormously since this was written this is still an informative description.

There are estimated to be many thousands of Intentional communities around the world. Some of which have survived and thrived for four or five decades, many new ones have been formed over the last thirty years or so and a significant new wave of interest in intentional communities has grown over the last several years. Although there is enormous diversity among intentional communities, many share land or housing, however, more importantly, their members usually share a common vision and work actively to carry out their common purpose.

The purposes of communities vary widely. Communities have been formed to share resources, to create great family neighborhoods, to live ecologically sustainable lifestyles, or to live with others who hold similar values. Some communities are wholly secular; others are committed to a common spiritual practice; many are spiritually eclectic. Some are focused on egalitarian values and voluntary simplicity, or mutual interpersonal growth work, or growing food and self-reliance. Some communities provide services such as helping war refugees, the urban homeless, or developmentally disabled children or adults. Some communities operate rural conference and retreat centers, health and healing centers, or sustainable-living education centers.

While some of today's communities can trace their roots back to the counterculture of the `60s and `70s, few today identify with the hippie stereotype given at that time. Most intentional communities are not communes, although some people mistakenly think so. It is probably more useful to use the term "commune" to describe a particular kind of intentional community whose members live "communally" in an economic sense--operating with a common treasury and sharing ownership of their property.

Most communities are multi-generational with most members ranging in age from 30 to 60, with some in their 20s, some 60 and older, and many children.

On the political spectrum, communitarians tend to be left of center. In terms of lifestyle choices, they are mostly hard working, peace loving, health conscious, environmentally concerned, and family oriented. Philosophically they tend toward a way of life, which increases the options for their own members without limiting the choices of others.

The most common form of governance is democratic, with decisions made by some form of consensus. Of the older communities that formerly followed one leader or a small group of leaders, most have changed in recent years to a more democratic form of governance.

Because communities are by definition organized around a common vision or purpose, their members tend to hold a lot of values and beliefs in common--many more than shared among a typical group of neighbors. Still, disagreements are a common occurrence in most communities, just as in the wider society. The object of community is not so much to eliminate conflict as to learn to work with it constructively.

The degree of privacy and autonomy in communities varies as widely as the kinds of communities themselves. In some communities individual households own their own land and house, and have their own independent economy (perhaps with shared facilities, as in many land co-ops); their degree of privacy and autonomy is nearly identical to that of mainstream society. However, in communities with specific religious or spiritual lifestyles (such as monasteries or some meditation retreats), privacy and autonomy are typically more limited, as part of the purpose for which the community was organized. Most communities fall between these two points on the privacy/held-in-common spectrum.

The trend among intentional communities forming now is toward more individual control than was common among those that were formed in the `60s and `70s. For example, one of the fastest growing segments of the community movement today is cohousing, where residents enjoy autonomy similar to that of any planned housing development. Finding a healthy balance between individual needs and those of the community is a key issue for the future in both intentional communities and the larger society in general.

Communities make a wide variety of choices regarding standard of living--some embrace voluntary simplicity, while others emphasize full access to the products and services of today's society. People within Intentional Communities tend to make careful choices about the accumulation and use of resources, deciding what best fits with their core values. Regardless of the choices made, nearly all communities take advantage of sharing and the opportunities of common ownership to allow individuals access to facilities and equipment they don't need to own privately (for example power tools, washing machines, vehicles, and in some cases, even swimming pools).

In terms of material wealth, communities often evolve like families: starting off with limited resources, new communities tend to live simply. As they mature, they tend to create a stable economic base and enjoy a more comfortable life--according to their own standards. Many established communities (20 years and older) have built impressive facilities, some of which are quite innovative in design and materials. The money to finance these improvements have often come from successful community businesses, ranging from light manufacturing to food products, from computer services to conference centers.

Many people choose to live in community because it offers a way of life, which is different, in various ways, from that of the wider society. Since living in community does not eliminate everyday responsibilities, most community members raise families, maintain and repair their land and buildings, work for a living, pay taxes, etc. At the same time, communitarians usually perceive their lifestyle as more caring and satisfying than that of mainstream culture, and because of this--and the increased free time which results from pooling resources and specialized skills--many community members feel they can engage more effectively with the wider society. In fact, many communitarians are deeply involved in their wider community of neighbors, and often provide staffing or even leadership for various local civic and social change organizations.

Perhaps the biggest area of growth in intentional communities these days is in the building of Ecovillages that is taking place all over the World. Many people are using the term 'Ecovillage' to describe their communities, their environmental building projects, and other endeavors.

Q

What is an 'Ecovillage'?

The Global Ecovillage Network: www.gen.ecovillage.org which was created following the Ecovillage Conference at the Findhorn Community in 1995, uses the following definition of an Ecovillage:

'Ecovillages are urban or rural communities of people, who strive to integrate a supportive social environment with a low impact way of life. To achieve this, they integrate various aspects of ecological design, permaculture, ecological building, green production, alternative energy, community building practices, and much more.'

This description makes it clear that an Ecovillage is made up of much more than eco-friendly building. It is a whole package that includes methods of energy production and energy saving, environmental approaches to waste management, wholesome and sustainable methods of food production and sustainable approaches to economic, social and community development.

A great deal of information about all these elements that have been developed in one Ecovillage is available at: www.ecovillagefindhorn.org. This site gives details of the Findhorn Wind Park, the living machine – natural sewage and wastewater management system, Earth-Share, this community's food production and community food share scheme, Ekopia, the Development Trust and Community Resource Centre, which is responsible for raising development funds and creating and managing the community's local currency.

> At the time of writing, the Findhorn Ecovillage has the lowest recorded ecological footprint for any community in the industrialized world, just half the UK national average.

A comprehensive education curriculum on design and education regarding Ecovillages can be downloaded for free at:
www.gaiaeducation.org/index.php/en/download-the-curriculum.html.

This Ecovillage Design Curriculum has been an official contribution to the United Nations Decade of Education for Sustainable Development

According to Tony Sirna in his piece: What is an Ecovillage? An Ecovillage is: *A vision, an ideal, a goal.*

He considers that:

Except for some villages within aboriginal cultures that have retained their ancient sustainable ways, there are no examples of fully realized Ecovillages as of yet and those using the term are describing a commitment or intent to live more sustainably, reintegrating their lives with ecology.

Beyond a shared commitment to sustainability, Ecovillages are diverse in many ways. They exist in rural, urban, and suburban areas and in all parts of the world, among a variety of cultures. They can be embedded in a larger human settlement, such as a neighborhood in a large city. They can be newly formed projects just under way, or older groups redefining themselves or hanging a new term on what they've been doing all along.

In general, the term Ecovillage is used to describe places that are aiming for a village-like quality. A village is more than just a place to live. A village is also a place for work and play, birth and death, trading of goods and services, celebrations, and all aspects of healthy lives. Equally important is being 'human scale,' meaning a population where it is still possible for people to know each other as individuals and not as anonymous masses.

I agree with Tony Sirna when he states that an Ecovillage is a process as well as a vision, and those who are involved in them are all somewhere on a long path. In many ways the same can be said of the process of creating an intentional community from scratch and also in Transitioning a Town or endeavoring to develop a greater sense of community spirit and engagement within a village, town or city district.

What is a culture for sustainability in communities?

Living things
Whether intentional or local, communities are living things; made up of multiple personalities, each contributing different perspectives, motivations, experience and skills. It is the combination of all of these that forms the character and the culture of a community. How well a community recognizes and manages these differences, utilizes the strengths and handles the weaknesses can determine how sustainable that community will be.

> Being actively involved in community sustainability is not only about learning new ways of doing things it is also about unlearning ways of being and doing that have created the social, cultural, environmental, economical and moral challenges and problems that are detrimentally affecting many societies.

> Communities are ideal situations in which people can develop themselves through learning or improving skills, especially in personal communication and co-operative working.

Communities thrive when their members have, or learn to develop, attitudes of tolerance, openness, mutual support and respect. It is becoming obvious to many people that by modeling and demonstrating these skills and attitudes within their communities they can have a positive influence upon society.

> What seems not to be so evident to many people is that it is mainly, perhaps only, when a society has these mutually beneficial skills and attitudes at its core that it is most likely to nurture its citizen's, protect the environment and be socially and financially sustainable.

> What is becoming clear to many of us searching for solutions to the problems facing most societies is that community is the answer, or, at least, a significant part of it.

For many of us, being a part of a group with some aims and intentions in common gives us strength. Strength to seek solutions to difficulties, challenges and problems and do so with mutual respect, supportive attitudes and good humor, while having a sense of belonging to a place and its people. Feeling that we a playing some part in the sustainability of such a group and such a place is empowering.

The seeds of sustainability

It is within a consciously maintained community process towards a vision of sustainability where the seeds of that sustainability are planted, cultivated, nurtured, blossom and bear fruit. These seeds are:

Being relevant

For any intentional community or community initiative to be sustainable it would need to have been relevant in the first place. Recognition of having real relevance in any situation can add strength to conviction and be a great aid to perseverance.

Clarity purpose and objectives

Having clarity of the purpose, intentions, aims and objectives will enable people to know what they are involving themselves in and will be essential yardsticks by which to measure outcomes and success.

Appropriate governance and leadership

Having the appropriate governance structure, legal identity and leadership systems will form a firm foundation upon which all other aspects of community can be built.

Agreement on values, ethics and behavior

Identifying the common ground of some shared values and ethics; the areas of commonality, and making agreements on these and upon attitudes and behavior can increase people's willingness for involvement within their community.

Conscious development of community culture

Consciously creating cohesion, encouraging cooperation and collaboration can improve relationships; enhance the quality of the community experience and save time, effort and resources.

Understanding the stages of community development

There is inevitability to the evolution of community culture and of the stages that any community is likely to go through in its development. Understanding this and perceiving what stage the community has reached in its development, and where the individuals within it are in their own development, will be supportive in successfully managing change and dealing with challenges.

Constructive communication

The quality of relationships within a community will be mostly determined by the quality of communication between the people involved. Communicating through clear, constructive speaking, self-disclosure, attentive and compassionate listening and direct, supportive feedback builds trust and underpins cooperation.

Creativity

Creativity in community means not only in all forms of the Arts and the built environment, it also means thinking outside the box, exploring new ideas and experimenting with potential solutions to all manner of challenges.

Celebration

Communities that celebrate together stand a good chance of staying together. The celebration of successes and of one another's achievements, anniversaries and rights of passage; the creation of new and the acknowledgement of old rituals and the marking of events of seasonal and religious significance lift spirits, brings richness and shared joy and delight.

Open discussion and inclusive decision-making

Being inclusive and thinking beyond personal needs in regular, well-managed and supportively facilitated meetings and discussions can move a community forward cooperatively. Consensus decisions achieved within sensible timeframes with agreed methods for progressing them can alleviate conflict and discontent.

Commitment, continuity and courage

Making commitments to one another, to the community, to the aims and objectives and the agreed values and ethics supports continuity. People can find it to be empowering to have the courage to embody these elements within themselves and in their community. Being willing to do all this in good times and, more importantly, in times of difficulty, can be a mark of maturity that could ensure sustainability.

Imaginative approaches to resources
Developing imaginative approaches to the acquisition and use of all resources, being creative through recycling, repairing and re-using materials will support ecological and economical sustainability.

Conscious awareness
Having the conscious awareness of the need to do each of the above, and demonstrating the willingness to do so, can make all the difference to the sustainability of any community.

Each of these topics will be covered in detail throughout this book.

2

BEING RELEVANT

The relevance of community-led regeneration

Many people around the world are becoming less prepared to put up with situations in their local communities that do not serve them well. They are often dissatisfied with the decisions that affect their lives that are made by others who have not taken their concerns, needs and views into consideration.

> People are discovering that they no longer feel powerless to influence the future of the communities in which they live.

They are getting together in groups large or small to bring about the changes they desire to see in their communities.

People attempting to influence decisions and improve amenities and services within local communities also find the mutual support resulting from grouping together with others with similar intentions gives them strength and provides sustainability for their initiatives. More and more people who understand the relevance of community engagement are willing to become involved in community projects and are stepping up to take some responsibility for making positive and beneficial change happen.

This is rarely done in isolation. Just at the time when it is important for people to become involved in creating the future they wish to see, there are ready-made mechanisms for sharing information and offering mutual support. Around the world there are many individuals, groups, organizations and communities with expertise and experience in community processes that can offer help. There are networks, local, national and global, through which useful information can be shared. There are movements such as Transition Towns, who offer information and tried and trusted formulas and models for community regeneration and particularly for increased local environmental sustainability: http://www.transitionnetwork.org.

It's clear that decisions made by a relatively few powerful or influential people - altruistic or self-interested – often do not properly address the needs and concerns of the majority of people struggling to make their lives work in the face of social, environmental and economic dysfunction.

> It makes far more sense for the people who are most effected to have a say in what is needed, to have a voice in the decision-making and a hand in the required actions.

The regeneration of a community requires involvement, input, discussion and decision-making by as wide a range of the community's citizens as possible. Community groups and organizations that have been formed for specific purposes can carry out many, and in some cases most, of the necessary activities, services and projects required within a community. Wise community groups will have an awareness of what other community groups are doing and will have the intention of being mutually supportive to one another.

Overcoming obstacles

Not everyone is happy with the idea of community empowerment. Some difficulties experienced by Voluntary and Community groups in the past have resulted from the attitudes of other people towards them when such groups emerge to deal with local problems; even when, or perhaps especially when, they seem to be doing so with success.

Perhaps people in public or private sectors responsible for some service provision might feel concerned that the service they have been providing may not compare favorably with a similar service being offered by an independent community group. People who hold positions of power and influence within the community or society may feel alarmed at the thought of citizens taking power into their own hands. Some might think that their own positions may be threatened, as is illustrated in the following story:

In 1995 I was part of a small group who initiated a project intended to bring the people in our town together to find solutions to a situation that had the potential for adversely affecting the future of our young people.

This was at a time when community-led initiatives; citizen involvement in community development and any form of community-led regeneration were in their infancy. No initiative of this nature or this scale and scope had previously been attempted in our region.

The project became increasingly difficult to gather momentum, despite the evident support and enthusiasm of many of the townspeople. Requests for small amounts of available public local funding and the use of local venues were declined. Original supporters began withdrawing their support without reason or with vague excuses. Reports appeared in the town's newspaper that questioned the motivation behind the project and indicated doubts about my character and integrity as the perceived leader of the project.

When my tenacity and persistence seemed apparently undiminished by all this I received, without warning, a notice of eviction from my little, rented cottage. My landlord, a member of the local village council, sent this notice by post giving the reason that by carrying out a business I was breaking my lease agreement. This 'business' was the voluntary coordination of the project.

I requested a conversation with the leading local politician who I learned was coordinating the efforts to prevent the project from proceeding. I asked him to tell me his reasons for undermining the initiative and making life difficult and uncomfortable for us. He replied. 'The trouble with you is that you're trying to give power to the people. People do not know what to do with power. They need folks like me,' he said, 'to make decisions for them or at least to limit their choices to those that will have as little effect as possible on how things are managed'.

The people of the town clearly didn't agree with him. They came together in the initiative and over time they created a large number of projects and programs that greatly improved life in the town and the potential for its future.

Whether the attitudes of people like this local politician are based on personal ambition or a misplaced sense of paternalism, the results are usually similar; the power and control in communities remain in the hands of the few, (some of whom are elected and some of whom have not received any mandate through the democratic process).

> I believe this to be an old paradigm that thankfully we are gradually evolving beyond.

Even so, during the time that has elapsed since that 1995 project, it seems apparent that, on the whole, we have not moved as far forward with community-led regeneration initiatives as might have been hoped for.

I recently came across a report, partially reproduced below, that succinctly sums up what is happening in many instances of community-led regeneration and what needs to happen to bring about real change. Although this report is in regard to Scotland, it could apply to many urban and rural communities in most developed countries.

A report on community-led regeneration

Government would acknowledge that in many cases approaches to community involvement, development and regeneration have either failed to deliver the desired outcomes or have been severely impaired. At the time of writing (04.10.2011) this is mostly attributed to the fundamentally changed economic circumstances within which potential regeneration has been taking place. (The global banking crisis of 2008.) One report indicates that 'Despite the substantial sums that have been invested in a variety of regeneration initiatives over a sustained period of time, the key indicators of social and economic disadvantage that triggered this investment in the first place have shown little signs of improvement'.

The conclusion to be drawn from the evidence of the past thirty years is that top down, physical regeneration does not, of itself, create long term and sustainable solutions to social difficulties. The assumption that underpinned many previous regeneration strategies is that it is the job of government, both national and local government working together, to resolve the complex sets of challenges facing our most disadvantaged communities. It seems clear that it is this assumption that now needs to be laid to rest if the challenge of how to deliver community-led regeneration is to be met.

While these communities are prime examples of community-led regeneration they all share a story in common, which describes many years of struggle in order to get to the stage of development that they are now at. In particular, all the community leaders involved would, in part at least, ascribe that struggle to varying degrees of opposition encountered from across a range of external stakeholders. While there may be some merit in the argument that the process of engaging in a struggle of some sort can forge a deeper level of commitment in the long term, the fact remains that much community-led regeneration has evolved as it has in spite of the attitude and behavior encountered from external stakeholders – rather than because of them.

Successful community-led regeneration should not be as difficult to achieve or as costly in human terms as it has proved to be in many cases. Nor should the whereabouts of the successful examples be as randomly haphazard and dependent on the fortuitous presence of key individuals or local circumstances. For any new regeneration strategy that places an emphasis on community-led regeneration, it will be essential that a more systematic and strategic means of achieving this is identified, which can also reduce the length of time that the process takes

Investing in community-led regeneration

If Government is committed to a regeneration strategy that is community led, then investment will be required to bring this about. It is worth noting that several existing policy initiatives that Government is already committed to are also geared towards communities taking on more responsibility and control over what happens at a local level. However, the successful implementation of all these policies is contingent on communities having a sufficient level of capacity and local organization in order to respond. Experience tells us that the required levels of capacity do not necessarily exist in every community – indeed in the areas of most severe disadvantage and where the regeneration challenges are greatest, the required levels of local capacity and organization are less likely to be present.

I understand the concerns stated in the last paragraph. However, from my experience, I have learned that in most groups, whether a handful of people or a whole community, there is, more often than not, most of what is required for the group or community to succeed in its purpose. In most cases there is also recognition of when additional skills need to be learned and when some expertise and experience might be beneficially sought from elsewhere. When some piece is missing there will usually be someone who knows somebody who could provide that piece.

> It would seem a sensible strategy for an initiating community group to have advisors on many subjects readily available to them.

Establishing networks among voluntary groups and projects around the community could provide further access to specialist knowledge in a variety of fields.

Essential training and the improvement of people's capacities would seem to be the most important areas in which to pay attention and for which to raise funds. Do you remember the saying?

'Give a man a fish and you feed him for a day. Teach him to fish and you will feed him for life.'

This is particularly relevant to building skills within communities.

> You Make the Difference participates in a scheme to share the useful and beneficial information in our books with people around the world who are endeavoring to make a difference within their communities. Visit www.skillsshare.net to learn how, with help from Amazon, you can easily make the difference to those community initiatives that you would like to help become sustainable.

A wise strategy would be to have open communication in all aspects of any community initiatives. This would obviously include minutes or records of all meetings about projects, regardless of with whom, to be made publicly and easily available. It also includes being open and direct when requesting information, asking questions and challenging decisions and behavior. Secrecy is usually for the protection of people who have something to hide. (A few locally influential people, some of whom had been publicly elected, who colluded with one another to protect the status quo, held, in secret, the meetings to create strategies intended to undermine our community initiative in 1996.)

> The demonstration of and the demand for open communication in all aspects of community discussion can shine a bright light in concealed places!

The reluctance of some people to support locally-led projects and regeneration initiatives might be out of genuine concern or with the best of intentions rather than for personal protection. Open and direct requests for clarification regarding such concerns and intentions will bring these out into the open for discussion and resolution.

Alliances

Many of us have come to realize that the most effective approach to dealing with bureaucracy or opposition to a community project is to create alliances with other groups. Although the needs of the various parties involved in the discussions regarding a community initiative might be quite different, the primary objectives are often compatible.

For example, a community project for promoting and developing the arts might require quite a large building in which to do this effectively. The outright purchase of such a building may be beyond the group's financial means. If a city or district Council has a large disused building, such as an old town hall or a school that has been replaced by a more modern building, it may be difficult for them to find enough tenants to make the upkeep of such a building financially viable. If an alliance is formed between the Council and the project they might find mutually supportive ways for the project to take over the building and relieve the Council of responsibility for it. Other stakeholder groups could be brought into the alliance to widen the interest and involvement and to encourage and ensure greater inclusivity.

Recognizing potential allies instead of seeing opposition changes the energy from negative to positive. It is astonishing to see the improvement that this can make to all aspects of any project. It is not necessary for allies to be friends or to change any of their individual principles. Those involved can maintain different opinions, views and ideologies from one another and yet still find ways to work together towards mutually advantageous outcomes.

It can sometimes be wise for allies to be recognized as such rather than considered to be friends. In some situations this might prevent accusations of disloyalty amongst those with strongly held opinions, views or beliefs. It can also go a long way towards preventing cliques of self-interested groups from forming, such as what is commonly known as 'Old Boys Networks'. Alliances can stimulate creative thinking and can transform 'us and them' attitudes into attitudes of 'together we can!'

Governmental support for community empowerment and renewal

It seems clear that government at all levels now needs to actively help local communities to do more for themselves.

For them to take part and to help decide what happens where they live; to get more involved in decisions about the services in their community and to become more involved in deciding what local amenities are needed and in managing local assets and resources.

To do this it is vital for governments - national, regional and local - to make it much easier for people in communities to have their say and to take a more active part in decision-making. It is important to find more or improved ways of listening to what local communities want and to explore with those people how they can help decide about local services such as schools, hospitals, support services, transport, local community centres and more.

There are many things that could be considered:

1.   Attention could be paid to creating more Community Councils and on how existing ones function. Community Councils are made up of volunteers who live in a local area. These can help to inform Local Councils and other public authorities what people in their communities think about things like local services and to help people in their communities get more involved in deciding about and managing local services.

2.   There is a need for devising some new ways of delivering services in the community and to make it easier for community organizations to help manage local services. In some places,

communities have a right to challenge a local service if it is not run well or it does not meet the needs of the local people. If the public authority that is responsible for a service agrees with the challenge, it will look for a different organization to run the service. Sometimes the community can apply for and be given responsibility to run the service.

3. There is a need for new thinking on how money is used in providing some local services. As we know, the money for local services comes from the taxes that people pay. The government gives money to local councils and other public authorities, like the health service, so they can use this for local services. Local communities need to have more of a say in how the money for local services is spent. The local council or public authority could allocate some of the money for local services to the local community and let them decide how it is spent.

4. There is a need for more ways of helping communities to own land and buildings in their area and to be able to use these to develop local activities, services and community businesses. In every community there are buildings and land that the community may want to own. In some areas the local community has a right to buy some of the land when it comes up for sale. This usually happens in the countryside, although currently rarely in towns and cities.

5. There is a need to find easier ways for the passing of public land and buildings to the community. Sometimes the local council or other public authority owns land or buildings that it has stopped using or that it does not use much. The local community could be given the right to ask for the land or building to be passed to the local community so they can use it.

6. There is also a need to find ways for making the best use of buildings, land and resources that are not used or not used enough. There is now a need for exploration on how these can be better used; how they might be used as dwellings or shops or to help deliver services to the community.

7. Sometimes only sections of public buildings are used or they are shut for part of the week. Some public resources like buses or meeting halls are only used for part of the week. The community might want to use these building or resources at other times and for other purposes.

8. Sometimes houses, shops and areas of land that are owned by public authorities, companies or individuals are empty and not used for a long time. This can cause problems in a local community and so ways need to be found to alleviate these problems, while, at the same time using these buildings and land for the public good.

9. Owners could work with the local council so that unused land or empty buildings are used again. If the owner cannot be found or does not want to do this, the local council could arrange for the land or buildings to be sold allowing them to be used effectively. Local communities could be given the right to ask the local council to arrange this so that the community can buy and use the land or buildings.

10. There is now a need to think of ways of using private land or buildings over a short time. Sometimes, people own land or buildings that are not currently being used although there might be a plan to use the land or buildings later. The owner could agree to let the community use the land or buildings for a short time. The community could then give the land or building back when the owner needs it. To do this the owner and the person or group using the land would sign a mutually acceptable agreement. Ways will need to be found to make it easier for landowners and communities to do this.

11. Through a choice for healthy living or as a result of financial circumstances, many more people want to grow some of their own food. Not everyone has a garden. Sometimes, people can get a piece of land from the local council so they can grow fruit and vegetables. In most places there are currently not enough of these allotments or gardens for everyone who wants one. Some of the unused land previously mentioned could be acquired for this purpose either purchased or leased long term by the community.

These are only a few of the ways in which governments at all levels can be more supportive of community sustainability and through which local communities can empower themselves. There are many other ideas and things that could be done to support people in communities to get more involved in local decisions and activities that will make a difference where they live.

> It only requires willingness from the various levels of Government and some creative thinking and enthusiasm from people in local communities to make a difference. It will also take commitment from all concerned. In my experience commitment has magic in it!

With the explosion of social media, wise politicians in all tiers of governance are now realizing that it is far more sensible to work with the people who elected them and not just for them - and certainly not against them out of fear for their own status or for personal advancement. Sensible people managing bureaucracy are now recognizing that supporting community development is essential and that supporting community-led regeneration is an effective use of time and resources.

Example of a community-led initiative

Here I relate further details of the previously mentioned 1996 community event and the projects resulting from it because it is an example of how the one small act of creating an opportunity for people to gather together in a way that encourages communication, creativity and commitment can have a profound effect on the future of a community or neighborhood and on everyone involved.

The following example might be inspirational to those people in villages, towns and cities who are embarking on initiatives to transform their communities into being more socially, economically and environmentally sustainable.

Future Search - Youth Matters

Everyone engaged in this event volunteered his or her time. Some handled administration and logistics before, during and after the event. Others ran the crèche, provided transportation or handled the catering (most of the food was donated by bakeries and other local food production companies). Many people were involved in fundraising to pay for the hire of the hall and other essential expenses. (Much of this funding would not have been required had local government been more appropriately supportive.)

Each person who represented one of the many stakeholder groups in the community: parents, teachers, young people, youth leaders, social workers, business leaders, police and Church leaders, either volunteered their time, persuaded their employers to give them leave of absence or to send them to the event as representatives. The Academy (Scottish

Secondary School) happily gave some pupils time off school to attend.

The facilitators of this event were professionals who were trained and accredited to facilitate the Future Search process. Believing in the potential of this community initiative, they collectively donated dozens of hours of facilitation time to the event. They asked only that their expenses be covered.

Over three remarkable days the participants first looked back at events over the past twenty years that had influenced the development of the town. They then considered current aspects of life in the town that they were proud of and those they were not so proud of. Then they dreamed into the most fabulous future they could imagine for their town and for their children. They came up with ideas for projects and initiatives that would create that future. They then made their individual and collective commitments to seeing those to fruition.

All of this resulted in many community projects that have helped the people of the town and the surrounding area in a multitude of ways. As well as an increased awareness for the need for more employment opportunities, the immediate results for the youngsters were the creation of a number of youth projects:

1. A skateboard park.
2. A youth café.
3. A mentoring scheme for adults with skills and experience to support and guide youngsters.

This event also led to the creation of other projects with wider community objectives:

a. A LETS System - local Exchange Trading Systems, which, for a time, was the fastest growing system of its kind in the world.
b. A project for repairing and rebuilding computers and associated equipment to be made available to people in the community who needed them. (This was 1996, when the scale of IT was not what it is today).
c. The Furniture Store, a project in which furniture and furnishings no longer required were collected and stored and then redistributed to people who needed them. (This proved invaluable when, a short while later, the river overflowed its banks damaging the contents of many homes.)

Probably the most significant initiative was the setting up of the Community Resource Centre – referred to as The Hub. Run from an empty shop just off the High Street, this became the place where people went for advice and information on such things as fundraising and other financial issues, project start-up and management, IT advice, training and networking, etc. Over the following years this helped with the initiation and sustainability of many community projects.

Over time, a more firmly established sense of community and cooperative working among people of different backgrounds has led to the startup of many more local projects. One of these was the High Street Regeneration Scheme. This was beneficial during the first years following a large national supermarket being built on the edge of the town. Another project was to conserve and protect several small pockets of natural beauty that surrounded the town. Yet another was the creation of a trail - a footpath, bridleway and cycle-path out into the countryside.

Although I know they did not anticipate it at the time, many of the volunteers in the Future Search event have benefitted directly or indirectly from their involvement. Many have formed lasting friendships based upon their shared experience and the mutual interests discovered. Some people learned much from this experience with which they have been able to improve their paid or volunteer work and some were later offered jobs in community organizations and local businesses. Others have been elected as representatives on local and regional councils.

The professional facilitators achieved a reputation through this event that has enabled them to facilitate this process in many other communities around the UK. For a number of years following this event the town was held up as an example of successful community involvement and cooperation.

The relevance of intentional communities

There are many reasons for starting or joining some type of intentional community:

a. To share a common interest.
b. To support one another in common ideals.
c. To fulfill a common need.
d. To share a common task.
e. To achieve a common objective.
f. To develop and manage a project.
g. To pool resources.
h. To share ideas, information and experience.
i. To provide mutual support.
j. To provide mutual safety.
k. To offer help to others.

Of these many reasons, ones of significance are companionable living and mutual support. Even the most individualistic of people, who may be totally focused upon their own goals, will usually fare better in a community that offers some form of mutual support.

> Comfort and strength can be gained from being in a supportive community and sharing some of life's challenges with other people who are dealing with similar circumstances or shared experiences.

Intentional communities have relevance for the people who may be exploring and experimenting with some alternative approaches to some aspects of life. These could include:

> ➢ Exploring new forms of education.
> ➢ Experimenting with social and governance structures, leadership and collective decision-making.
> ➢ New economics, financial exchange, business practices, and relationships.
> ➢ Investigating and developing alternative and complementary health practices and methods for offering therapeutic support.
> ➢ Yoga and meditation.
> ➢ Organic food production.
> ➢ Building Ecovillages and Cohousing projects and other approaches to ecological and environmental sustainability.

Over the last few decades the attitudes of exploration, creativity and commitment to these within intentional communities have expanded the boundaries of understanding on these topics and have proven and demonstrated their benefits and value.

Even so, some of these approaches, attitudes and activities within international communities have often been ahead of their time and in the past some have been considered by traditional thinkers to be odd, even laughable. And yet, much of this radical thinking has now become mainstream. Although still on the cutting edge in some areas, the experimentation conducted in many intentional community 'Petri dishes' and the demonstration of the results are now considered in many places around the planet to be common sense, extremely relevant and obvious solutions to local and global problems.

> In many cases these explorations and demonstrations of community living within intentional communities have been inspirational and supportive to many people endeavoring to develop and sustain local communities.

Community relevance during crises

It is becoming apparent that in the coming years our societies could be at increasing risk from any number of potential crises. Ecological instability, economic meltdown, the depletion of non-renewable resources and energy reserves, major natural disasters, unstoppable epidemics, terrorism and possibly much more. Most of us will be aware that any serious, dangerous or life-threatening crisis can bring out the best and the worst in all of us.

When a crisis adversely affects us in our localities how are we likely to behave towards the people around us that we do not know and whose background, experiences and way of life we may not understand? How will we behave when we feel at risk, vulnerable and afraid? Who will we turn to for help and support when we live among strangers if systems stop functioning or society collapses?

We might be able to avert demonstrating the worst in us if we have already made conscious effort to get to know the people who live around us; have learned to understand one another, to have moved past our differences, developed friendships and mutual trust. Knowing that we are part of a community, local or intentional, might help to bring out the best in us; even in the most challenging circumstances.

> Communities can have real relevance and significance for those of us who are now realizing that community is the solution to many of society's current and potential future problems.

Identifying the relevance and need for a community project

When considering creating a local community project it is wise to establish if there is a real need for such a thing and if there is sufficient interest in the idea from people essential to its success.

Important questions to consider

Before starting, it would be wise to carefully consider the following questions:

    A. What is the purpose?
    B. What is the reason?
    C. Is there a genuine need for it?

D. Who is interested in participating?

E. Are they properly prepared to be part of it?

F. Could your proposed initiative become a part of one that already exists?

G. Could you work cooperatively with or alongside another initiative?

> Clearly stating your objectives will help you and other people to understand what to expect from your project and what you and they can offer to it.

A. What is the purpose of this project?

It is important to be aware of and to be clear about the purpose of any project right from the start. This is essential for attracting the appropriate people and necessary resources and support. If the initiators are not clear about the purpose then how can other people be?

B. What is the reason for creating this initiative?

Being clear about the reasons for creating a project can save a lot of time and effort and can make it obvious what strategies will be needed. These reasons might be important to the initiator yet not so to other people. If the reasons are only of real interest to the initiator then the idea or project might not attract the people or support it needs.

On the other hand, a person with a great deal of passion for creating a project can inspire engagement and support from enough other people.

C. Is there a genuine interest in creating this?

In my experience, having established some idea of what the initiative is intended to achieve and the reasons for its initiation, it is vital to ensure that there is a real interest for it.

There are many similarities in starting a project to that of starting a business. The failure of some businesses occurs when the enthusiasm of the proprietors is greater than the real need for their product or service. This also applies to the interest in community.

The first essential step is to do some research into the viability of the project by assessing the interest in the idea. It is surprising how frequently initiatives are initiated to fulfill some purpose that has not been properly thought through. It is surprising how frequently work is embarked upon to create a project when hardly any research has been done or for which there is little recognizable need or interest.

Whose need is it?

Over the years, I have become aware that occasionally the desire of some individuals can be more about their own needs than any real requirement for something to exist. Such a need might be for some kind of support that would specifically benefit their own situation or perhaps that of a relatively few people.

It could be sensible to carry out an assessment of the real size of the need or interest in a project. If choosing to continue, it might be wise to scale its size to fit the size of the actual need. I have seen situations where the setting up of an initiative that was larger than necessary proved to be an unsustainable use of time, effort and resources.

Establishing the need

One method of establishing if there is a need for your project is to conduct a survey. Surveys and questionnaires could become part of listening to the people within your community, especially those whom your project is intended to serve. This might require a widely conducted survey or involve one-to-one interviews with key people and stakeholder groups in the local area to identify needs and concerns and to discover what is already being done to establish a greater sense of community. The results of these will inform your strategies and activities.

Some suggestions for designing a survey questionnaire:
a. Be clear about what it is that you want to know, the reasons for the survey and what you want to learn from it.
b. Be inclusive in your survey in order to get as representative a spread of opinion as possible.
c. Make the questionnaire short and concise because most people are busy and are unlikely to be happy to answer endless questions.
d. Use simple, plain and accessible language. Avoid jargon and complex or lengthy questions.
e. Avoid asking leading questions.
f. For the integrity of the survey to be fully respected keep the tone as impartial and unbiased as possible.
g. Try a questionnaire out on a few people first to iron out any oddities, any questions that are confusing or which don't make sense.

There is skill in designing an effective questionnaire and just as much in collating and understanding the collected data. This might be an occasion to bring in someone with this skill and knowledge around statistics. This might be a role for one of your advisors or someone wanting to gain experience in this field.

The first community survey that I commissioned was written, conducted and processed by a volunteer final year student looking for field experience. She did a brilliant job; we received vital information and she gained the experience she needed for her dissertation. Win-Win!

Other research

It could be wise to also gather information about people's opinions, attitudes and expectations of a community initiative. You could conduct interviews to explore through a series of questions what those people intending to be involved would perceive as being successful. You might also organize some focus groups for brainstorming what people would consider to be indicators that a project was being a success or not. You will then have these against which to measure success and sustainability.

D. Who is already attempting to deal with this need?

This is important to recognize. Any attempt to start a community project in an area that is already well served by others could limit the effectiveness of your project. It might also divert much-needed resources from the established initiative. By creating unnecessary competition for limited resources you might be creating more problems than solutions.

E. How well are they doing?

It might be vital to your success to check out how well an existing similar community initiative is doing. You may discover that it is successfully achieving what you would hope to do. In which case starting another one may undermine their success and limit the possibilities of your own.

If it seems they are not doing very well it would be wise to investigate the reasons for that. You might discover that the reasons are outside their control. Lack of any real interest or support, restrictive regulations, or other difficulties and obstacles that are limiting their success could very well limit yours.

Q

F. Could you be a part of what they are doing?

Could your proposed initiative become a useful part of one that already exists? You might not need to create another initiative if your skills and enthusiasm could be offered and accepted by an existing project.

Q

G. Could you work cooperatively with another initiative?

Could your proposed initiative work co-operatively with, alongside and in support of one that already exists? If an existing project is successfully doing what you want to do could you add to their success by contributing your own skills and experience?

If the people in an existing initiative are not managing to achieve what you want to achieve is it possible that they might be able to do so if they had the benefit of your experience, skills and support?

> If the benefits of a community initiative are not obvious – or are only so to one person; if there is currently little enthusiasm for such a project, and, if other similar community initiatives are already in existence locally, it would be sensible to give some careful thought and consideration to the wisdom of launching your initiative.

If, after doing all of this research, you are convinced that your idea for a community or initiative is needed and has every chance of being successful and sustainable then get started on planning your strategies; letting your intentions be known and attracting the members and support that you need.

If the membership of the group to support this initiative has not yet been identified, this would be the time to do that.

3

STARTING UP

Whether creating an intentional community or a community initiative, there are two ways to start:
1. Just get on and do it.
2. Do some strategic planning.

The first is based on the premises that once something is up and running it is much easier for people to see the benefits and to consider how they could help and get involved. It is often easier to get cooperation and support for something that people can see is working, or has potential, than it is to persuade people to an abstract concept of community. Especially if people have no personal experience of an intentional community; if you have been thinking outside the box or come up with a concept that some people might have difficulty grasping, or in which they might only see limitations or problems.

> Just getting on with it can be an effective way to establish a small community or project for which there is a lot of enthusiasm from a sufficient number of committed people.

Sometimes the start of the regeneration of a local community or the improvement of the sense and spirit of community begins with a single initiative that inspires community engagement. Perhaps a project idea is so simple and easy to start that no forward planning is involved; people just get on and do it.

Occasionally, such a project has an immediate effect upon a community that it takes on a life of its own and grows way beyond the original concept. An example of this is the Incredible Edible project in the little town of Todmorden in the North of England.

Incredible Edibles

This community initiative was started by a small group of people who wanted places to grow food in their local area for consumption by the local community.

In this town there was very little spare land available for this project and so the group just started planting in whichever spaces seemed appropriate – and some places that might be considered by some to be not appropriate at all!

This project has changed the way this small town looks and eats. Food is now grown all over the place, in every imaginable - and several unimaginable places around the town. People who have never grown anything before have discovered the joy of growing things and realized that they have green fingers. Children now know where their fruit and vegetables come from and how they are grown. The cost of fruit and vegetables has come down and the consumption of healthy food has gone up. In this small town that was founded during the industrial revolution there is greenery everywhere and an abundance of fresh food for the picking.

The founders of that project talk about the organic nature of the development and expansion of their project – perhaps appropriate for a gardening project! They explain that they had an idea and just got on with it. They simply started planting in disused or little used areas of the town. This inspired others to join in and the project seemed to take on a life of its own.

They learned what they needed to learn as they went along and the people with whatever skills had become necessary just turned up or were easily coaxed into participating. As the project spread throughout the town, became more complex, and perhaps larger than first envisioned, systems were devised and put into place to manage whatever needed to be managed.

These people enthusiastically extol the virtues of just getting on with making the difference that is desired or necessary and see what happens!

Check the website for a tool-kit, loads of other information and especially for inspiration: http://www.incredible-edible-todmorden.co.uk

This can be an effective way to establish a project for which the need or benefit is obvious, for which there is a lot of enthusiasm, and where nothing similar already exists.

Planning

When starting most intentional communities or local initiatives, some strategic planning is useful and for many, will be essential, especially if money is involved or there are legal requirements to be met.

> For many people, the most exciting aspects of starting a community are the envisioning of its potential, the planning for its development and the creation of systems and structures to support the activities and ongoing sustainability.

An efficient, effective and fun way to engage in some planning and kick-start any project is to follow the example set by the inspirational people in Good for Nothing:

Good for Nothing!

This is a group of thinkers, doers, makers and tinkerers applying their skills and energy to accelerating the work of cause-led innovators and change makers. It is about diverse groups of people collaborating together, working in new, faster, fun and better ways. It is about working with ideas and people that are leading the way to what a flourishing 21st-century society might look like.

Good for Nothing works in 2 main ways: firstly, through 4 to 48 hour think/hack/do creative, collaboration events; and secondly through web-based missions and an emerging web platform.

Good for Nothing is a growing group of smart folk who collaborate with social innovators, social business and enterprise, activists, change makers, filmmakers and charities. The group welcomes anyone with skills who has a desire to get stuck in.

Those involved give time, money and energy to do stuff that supports people trying to make a positive impact and change. They are doing this through creative, collaborative gigs. These bring together a large diverse community of talented people to work with grassroots, cause-led social innovators in a playful, competitive, experiential experience lasting between 4 and 48 hours.

Good for Nothing is about bringing these people together and seeing what happens. It's also about exploring fun, open, collaborative and self-organized ways of working.

Good for Nothing is founded on 3 core practices:

1. Doing, not talking

It's not hard to talk clever and think big and there's an oversupply of that in our world. Too often big thinking doesn't lead to big doing. We look around and see so much that needs doing. Roll up your sleeves and 'fail gloriously' as Duke Stump once said. Good for Nothing stands for permission to have a go, get involved, participate, and to try stuff.

2. Collaboration and experimentation

Words we all hear a lot, however, true collaboration is where real diversity and openness is welcomed, where we let go of power and control, where we self-organize and allow ideas and energy to emerge more naturally and where we prototype and develop them rapidly. We want to do more of that.

3. Support the true innovators

Give creative energy to the real innovators who are trying to make positive change happen. When we look around for social, environmental and human innovation, a lot of the most exciting stuff is happening at the grass roots. We provide creative support to those pioneers. We think that can help accelerate positive change and impact.

The Rules of the Game at the events are:

1. Having up to 48 hours to do good for nothing.
2. Break the rules and see how far you can get.
3. Be useful. When you aren't; move on. If you can help other teams - do.
4. There is no expert panel; everyone say's what they love.
5. This doesn't need to stop tomorrow!

Learning by doing has become a bit of a mantra at the Good for Nothing base camp. The result has often been hectic, occasionally bonkers but always an incredibly exciting rollercoaster ride for the growing community of good for nothings. See more on the website: http://www.goodfornothing.com/about/

By being and doing good for nothing, anyone with skills and expertise can help with the startup of intentional communities or in creating a greater sense of community in local areas.

Creating strategies for remaining relevant and sustainable

> It is my experience that communities and initiatives are most often effective when there is commitment, clear intention, careful planning, sensible thinking, direct requests for what is needed and openness to possibilities. Communities thrive if, right from the start, sufficient attention is paid to inclusivity, to creating community cohesion and making conscious efforts to maintain it.

It is important to remember that some communities might not survive for very long without some conscious attention being given to all this. Even though communities and initiatives might continue for some time, and although they may achieve many of their objectives, their interactions and activities could be full of friction and disharmony and offer little pleasure to their members, of which there might be a constant turnover.

In any community or project it is important to develop strategies for achieving a variety of objectives. Different strategies will be required at different times.

Strategies will be needed for the following aspects:

Identifying the intention, purpose and objectives.

At the start of any community or initiative it is wise to identify the purpose and objective aims, goals, desired outcomes and results and the appropriate ways of working together. When these are all clear, the strategies for creating the most direct path towards these usually become obvious.

Creating structures

Deciding upon and working within appropriate legal, financial, management and leadership structures is vital for clarity, smooth running and the sustainability of a community or initiative, as is effective meeting management and inclusive decision making.

Finding people

Whether a community has an identifiable membership, a group made up entirely of volunteers or an organization with some paid staff and some volunteers, there will be a regular need for new people to replace those who leave or to help with the expansion of work. It will be wise to have strategies in place for identifying and recruiting the necessary and appropriate people and for encouraging engagement by as many people as possible covering a wide range of skills and experiences.

Creating the culture

In creating a culture for community sustainability the strategies would include establishing ethics and values and making agreements around these and around ways of being together and behaving towards one another; understanding of community development; appropriate attitudes towards leadership; developing procedures for maintaining cohesion and cooperation, for creative thinking, celebrating together and supporting one another's courage and commitment.

Good communication

How people in any community speak and listen to one another will have a significant impact upon the quality of cooperation, collaboration and cohesion. Using the simple elements of Constructive Communication as the basis for all interpersonal communications will help to develop good relationships, build trust, avoid misunderstandings and can save time, effort and money.

Achieving outcomes

In terms of achieving the desired outcomes, the strategies would be to identify the best ways for achieving the objectives, the means for acquiring any necessary resources – people, funding, equipment and services - and pay attention to the plans for each step and for who will do what, how, where and when.

Dealing with difficulties

Some difficulties may be specific to each community or initiative and others will be general and applicable to most community situations.

Creating the above strategies can alleviate and perhaps prevent many difficulties from arising. However, it is inevitable that things will go wrong from time to time. The trick is to be aware when this is happening by paying attention and through feedback systems and complaint procedures. Have strategies for investigating what is going wrong, taking immediate action to put things right, dealing with conflict and learning from the experience.

Measurement and evaluation

It would be sensible to have strategies in place for monitoring, measuring and evaluating progress.

Measurement and evaluation

These are essential to ensure that any community is achieving its desired objectives; that the systems, procedures and processes are being appropriately effective and that people involved are content with progress. To maintain the project's effectiveness and continued relevance the strategies would include methods for monitoring activities; measuring and evaluating results; procedures for gaining feedback; and establishing ways of estimating continued relevance. It would also be wise to create exit strategies for when any project has achieved its objectives.

It would be wise to consider the following questions, especially if your community has an intention to bring about a change and to make a difference to people or to a situation:

1. How will you measure progress and success?
2. How will you know how effective you are being?
3. How will you establish what affect you are having?
4. How will you recognize if any thoughts and opinions have been changed by your efforts?
5. How will you measure satisfaction in the project of the people involved?
6. How will you measure their sense of achievement and fulfillment?
7. How will you measure the potential for sustainability?

Measuring progress isn't always a high priority at the start of an intentional community or during the beginning of an effort to increase a sense of community locally. However, creating simple and straightforward ways of gathering data will not only help with monitoring and measuring progress, it can be used to encourage support and be included in funding applications.

It would be wise to keep a record of all the activities and events in the community.

Options:

a. Record the number of people who were involved in community projects and what the outcomes have been.

b. Community working groups could be asked to record information that emerges from their work.

c. It could also be interesting and useful to make a photographic record of progress.

d. To avoid wasting time and resources it would be sensible to have ways for monitoring results of trainings and on the introduction of new systems or processes to check for their effectiveness. This could be achieved through surveys and by requesting and recording feedback from those involved.

Most of us live in a world where success is measured, more often than not, by financial profitability and economically beneficial outcomes. However, successes of community initiatives and of intentional communities usually have more than one bottom line. These usually include:

1. Ecologically sustainable and the raising of environmental awareness.

2. Improvement in people's health and well-being.

3. Increased collaborative community engagement.

4. Improvement of cooperation and social interactions between the people involved.

Intention

Commitment has magic in it; and so does strong intention.

I have seen things materialize, seemingly effortlessly, purely from the intention of a strong-minded individual or group. However, it would seem wise to support a strong intention with some sensible strategic planning and pro-activity.

Visualization

Have a clear vision for what you want to achieve and then imagine achieving it.

Make the image of success bright, colorful, exciting, interesting, and enjoyable. See the people you want to be involved happily, cooperatively and effectively engaged in achieving the objectives. Hold onto this vision through thick and thin and embellish it from time to time. As each stage of success is accomplished take time to enjoy and to celebrate that success.

The Ideal Day exercise described later in this book could help with this visualization process, which can be done alone or with others.

Openness

> Openness is an antidote to secrets and misinformation, to restricted thinking and to feelings of separation and elitism.

The most effective communities and initiatives are open in their communication with one another and with others. They are open to suggestions, to new ideas and new or different ways of thinking and doing things. They are also open to people joining in at any time who have the skills, experience, contacts or attitudes that would be beneficial.

Purpose

For a community or initiative to fulfill its purpose and achieve its objectives it is important that everybody involved is clear what that purpose and those objectives are and to be in agreement with them. These might be obvious and be what people have been attracted to support. On the other hand, they may be vague or not clear to some people. It is surprising how often the purpose, goals, the aims, the intentions and objectives of communities are unclear; even to many of those involved in them. These objectives can sometimes be a vague sort of understanding among some people and even a wish, a dream or an ideal among others.

The fact that people have already come together to create or join a community or project might indicate what those objectives and intentions are likely to be. However, because nobody thinks quite like anybody else, there could be differing versions or a variety of thoughts about these. In their eagerness to show that they are doing something, people within communities might confuse movement with appropriate action.

> Time spent in establishing the objectives and identifying ways in which they will be achieved can save huge amounts of wasted time and effort in the future.

Compatibility

It is important that the objectives of the individuals are compatible with stated aims of the community. Individuals can check this when considering joining a community or taking part in a project by asking those involved what the stated objectives are:

Q

> Are these aims written down?
> Is there a mission statement?
> Are there minutes of meetings that record a clear statement of intent?

When joining a community or project it might be wise to ask some existing members what each of them believes the stated objectives are and how the community is doing in achieving them.

If the goals have never been stated clearly or if some in the community disagree about what they are, someone asking for clarity might help to improve awareness about this. If the objectives are uncertain or unclear it is up to individuals to decide whether this is a community to which they wish to commit time and energy.

> When those in an established community invite new people to join them, effort could be saved and misunderstandings avoided if the objectives of the community are clearly stated for the benefit of the prospective members. Those people could then be asked to support those objectives.

Statement of intention, purpose and objectives

This ought to be a statement that best describes the community or the initiative and clearly shows the intended purpose and objectives.

Such a statement might be part of the articles of Association of the community or project. It could form the strap-line under the name of a community or an organization or it could be referred to in the Mission Statement.

"You Make the Difference is a virtual, global, Social Enterprise offering supportive information, free guides and inexpensive books and e-books that can help people to make a positive difference to their lives and to their communities."

Mission statements

Having a mission statement or statement of purpose helps people to understand immediately what a community or an organization does. This statement needs to be clear, unambiguous and concise. Whatever this statement is called, ideally, it ought to be succinct and easily remembered.

Sometimes the statement of objectives is the same as the statement of purpose and sometimes it needs to be created separately and in more detail.

> Creating a clear statement that describes the community or the initiative and its purpose ought to be done with many or all of those involved. People feel far more committed to something that they have had a hand in creating. So finding the words that encapsulate the essence of the community would best be done through a community process.

Words have power

Words are remarkably powerful. They have the power to persuade, to encourage, to include and to inspire people. They also have the power to alienate. It would be wise to carefully choose the words of your statement.

The community processes chosen to produce this statement ought to include opportunities for thinking out loud, for being creative and expansive and then refining and defining ideas. Brainstorming and Refining and any other process that allow everyone to have a say would be helpful. Many of these can be found in the books: ENJOYABLE & EFFECTIVE MEETINGS and EFFORTLESS FACILITATION in the YOU MAKE THE DIFFERENCE series, available from Amazon and accessible through: www.youmakethedifference.net.

Additional Objectives

Although there is usually one obvious objective, there may be some additional aims that could be very important – such as the attitudes within the community, in what spirit living and working will be done, and what else might be achieved along the way. To bring everyone on board it may be helpful to go through a refining process in which the essence of all these aims can be distilled and included.

An example of a succinct yet encompassing statement is that of Auroville, an intentional international community in South East India:

Auroville, a universal city in the making

"Auroville wants to be a universal town where men and women of all countries are able to live in peace and progressive harmony above all creeds, all politics and all nationalities. The purpose of Auroville is to realize human unity."

Another example is that of the Aims and Objectives of Transition Town Totnes:

Our Purpose

Transition Town Totnes (TTT) exists for the people of Totnes and District to help create thriving, healthy, caring local communities where people's ways of life take into account the needs of future generations as well as the present ones.

> Statements of purpose and of aims and objectives can sometimes be so lengthy and involved that they lose their punch.

Instead of being clear and concise these statements can be muddled and complex. Rather than engaging people such statements might lose their interest. The common cause of this is usually an attempt to come up with a statement that pleases all the people involved. This can be difficult to achieve when the membership of a community includes people with predominantly differing ways of receiving and processing information and for whom different words have special meaning and power.

Visual, Auditory and Kinesthetic people

> Although we each use most of our senses to learn - to recognize, receive, process and retain information - most of us have one mode that is predominant: Visual, Auditory or Kinesthetic.

Visual people

These people prefer to receive their information visually. They like to see things and often think in pictures. Symbols have power for them and they can take in a lot of information from a picture or a graphic image. These people are often visually creative. They usually have an eye for good design and often have good color sense. When expressing ideas, a predominantly visual person may often use expressions such as: 'I see... It looks as if... I noticed that...' Their speech will be peppered with visually descriptive words.

Auditory people

These people prefer to receive their information through words and sounds. They learn best through reading and listening and can usually remember much of what they hear and read. Predominantly auditory people are often musical and creative with the written word. When expressing ideas, a predominantly auditory person might use expressions such as: 'I hear that... It sounds as though...' Their speech will contain auditory descriptive words.

Kinesthetic people

These people mostly receive their information through experiences and feelings. They like to learn through experiencing and doing. Predominantly kinesthetic people are often attracted to professions and pastimes where they can express their feelings or demonstrate care. They might be involved in dance, theatre and tactile forms of self-expression; body work such as massage, and supportive activities like counseling. When expressing ideas, predominantly kinesthetic people might use expressions such as: 'I feel that... I have a sense that...' The words they use can be heavily biased towards those of emotions.

Putting it all together

When creating a statement of description, purpose and objectives, predominantly visual people are likely to want it to conjure up a visual image in the mind; auditory folk may prefer detailed written information and those with strong kinesthetic tendencies might desire the statement to evoke emotion.

Too much emphasis on any one of these modalities can turn off people with other predominant modes. For example, communities and groups in the fields of spirituality, healing or some aspects of personal growth can attract a high proportion of kinesthetic people. However, statements of objectives that have been put out by some of these have been considered by non-kinesthetic people to be at best 'warm and fuzzy'; at worst, too 'flaky' to be taken seriously.

> Creating a concise statement using some elements from each of the Visual, Auditory and Kinesthetic language modes is likely to have the most impact upon the greatest number of people.

It is worth remembering that for a community or an initiative that has been or is being newly formed this process itself can deepen relationships, bind people together and help everyone involved to have a good understanding of the whole picture.

4

THE PEOPLE

People are any community's biggest asset; without people there is no community!

Identify the appropriate people

Identify the people who have the skills and experience that are needed for success and sustainability. Seek out the most appropriate people and invite them to join the project or community. Some of those people might be known to you and may already be good friends with you and/or with one another.

Be inclusive

It may seem that a community or group formed of nice, friendly people who you know well and who like one another would make up the ideal group to work together harmoniously and cooperatively.

However, no matter how pleasant the prospect may be of being with friends, if there are not enough people who have the knowledge and experience needed then this might not result in the best outcome for the project.

When creating a sustainable community or community initiative it will be the appropriate skills, experience, contacts and essential qualities of those involved that are needed.

There may be some skills that you know to be essential to success yet you do not know anyone with those skills. Find out who has them! Ask around! Talk it over with the people already committed to the project. Put the word out in your community. Some great networking is done amongst communities and somebody in these networks will know just the people you need to approach.

Some of the people whose skills, experience or contacts you recognize would be useful to the project may be total strangers. Ask them to help anyway. People will say either yes or no. They may have personal reasons for saying no, such as time restraints, or they may not fully understand your vision or recognize the need for the project. Respect their decision. Even if they say no now, they may say yes later, when the project is more established.

It could save time and effort to develop a clear strategy for attracting community members and volunteers for the future when there will probably be an ongoing need for new people to replace those who leave or to help with an expansion of work. The strategy options for attracting volunteers set out in our book EMPOWERING VOLUNTEER MANAGEMENT could be helpful with this.

> Supportive, encouraging and positive people are invaluable in any community.

Membership

In intentional communities where people live and work closely together in an identifiable and specific structure and culture, it would be wise to have strategies in place for clarifying what constitutes membership, what are the rights and responsibilities of membership, and how these will be conveyed to prospective members. From my experience I have observed some unfortunate consequences upon their potential for sustainability when communities have no such strategies in place.

In my role as Listener Convener to the Findhorn Community it was my delightful task (usually!) to meet, greet, interview and welcome many potential new members. As well as implementing some of the above suggestions, I found it beneficial to all concerned to ask potential members a number of questions:
1. Why did they want to join this community?
2. What expectations did they have for being involved?
3. What skills and experience could they offer to the community?
4. How willing were they to do so?
5. What concerns or reservations did they have about living there?
6. Was there anything about themselves they wished to disclose?

This last question gave people the opportunity to demonstrate honesty and openness regarding anything with which they may need some support and/or of which the community ought to be aware.

It is wise to remember that joining an intentional community, Ecovillage or Cohousing project is often very similar to becoming a member of a large family. I have noticed that within communities, as in families, it is often out of the ignorance of the facts that problems arise. With this in mind it can be beneficial to have people with the appropriate skills, qualifications and experience to hold awareness roles in such areas as health and well-being, and safety and security, and to have strategies in place for dealing effectively with problems arising in these areas.

Making relationships

Having a regular flow of people joining and leaving a community, especially an intentional community, can result in a sense of impermanence and lack of continuity, which may affect sustainability.

It can also be a major factor in preventing people from developing friendships or meaningful relationships and from making commitment to one another.

One of the most precious gifts that I received during my 18 years in the Findhorn Community was learning how to deal with the arrival and departure of people in the community, and in my life.

Many thousands of people have been involved with this community since it was founded in 1962. Only a handful of people have been there for the majority of the time. The average length of time for living there has increased over the years since the development of the eco-village, which has enabled people to build or buy their own homes and settle down within the Community. However, many people still come to explore community living for a short time – weeks, months or years – and then move on to explore elsewhere; go back to their own homes; or begin forming their own community somewhere else.

Because the Findhorn Community is a centre for education and experimentation in community living this may be an extreme example of the movement of people through a community. Even so, most communities, intentional or otherwise, will have to deal with people arriving and leaving. How this is done can have an effect upon community morale and on sustainability. This can be greatly helped by cultivating the following attitudes within the community to new arrivals:
  ➢ Welcome them.
  ➢ Help them to quickly feel part of the community.

➢ Respect and appreciate them for who they are.
➢ Offer friendship.
➢ Show affection.
➢ Refrain from having unreasonable expectations of them.
➢ Be grateful for any contribution they make to community life.
➢ Celebrate and rejoice in any successes they achieve during the time they are in the community.
➢ Have no attachment to them staying.
➢ When they leave, release them with appreciation and best wishes for their future.

Most importantly, make genuine effort to unreservedly develop good social and/or working relationships and friendships.

Make total commitment to them as though these people will be in your life forever, which of course may turn out to be the case. This is not about being intense or forcing yourself on unsuspecting, and perhaps cautious people. Nor is it about being ingenious. It is about living in the moment, really connecting with people; becoming a friend and showing affection; fully enjoying the company of people, regardless of how long the relationship may last.

Wendell Berry, American activist, writer and farmer, wrote this about sustainability as it applies to small communities; he says it requires a 'continuously turning cultural cycle'.

"The cultural cycle is an unending conversation between old people and young people - assuring the survival of local memory; as long as it remains local - this has the greatest practical urgency and values. This is what is meant - and is all that can be meant - by 'sustainability'. The cultural cycle turns on affection; the primary motive for good care and good use is always going to be affection - because affection involves us entirely."

Volunteering in community

Many intentional communities and all local community-led initiatives depend heavily, sometimes entirely, upon people volunteering their time, expertise and experience for the community's benefit.

Volunteering is becoming an important aspect of many people's lives. Most of us are always ready to assist our friends and neighbors who occasionally need a helping hand and we are quick to step forward when help is required after some local catastrophe such as fire or flood. We might not think of this as volunteering; instead, we may consider it to be just helping out.

Many people want to contribute some of their time and talents in their local community or to an intentional community whose work they wish to support. Some people volunteer because they observe a need that they could help with or they identify a useful role that they could fill. Often, people are moved to volunteer for emotional reasons. Their hearts are stirred by compassion for others or a desire to help improve situations and circumstances. There are those for whom volunteering is a source of interest or an opportunity for spending time with other people. For others, volunteering can be a stepping-stone towards employment.

> Volunteering in community situations can be simple, effective, rewarding, immensely valuable and very enjoyable.

I have met many people who would like to volunteer in their community and yet have no idea about what they could contribute; a surprising number of these people believe they have no skills or useful experience to offer.

> I have never met anyone without some skill or experience that could be useful in most community situations.

There is a self-coaching process in the book, ENJOYABLE AND VALUABLE VOLUNTEERING, in this series that would help anyone to identify the skills and experience which, when volunteered, would be of benefit in a community situation. Some people who have engaged in this process have identified long lists of their skills, interests and experience that they could usefully volunteer. This process also helps with time management to identify ways of freeing up time for volunteering, and methods to support people to achieve and maintain high levels of excellence in their volunteering and to care for themselves while doing so.

Volunteer does not mean amateur

> It is vital for volunteers in any community situation to take their responsibilities seriously.

Even though volunteers are not being paid for the work they carry out, that does not diminish the importance of that work. It does not mean that they can turn up late when volunteering or be over casual, careless or slipshod when they get there. People will be relying upon them to do what they are required to do when they are needed to do it. A casual approach to their work by any volunteer could damage the reputation for professionalism that so many people have worked hard to establish in the Voluntary and Community Sector.

> Volunteers can help maintain this reputation and make the difference by helping to change any outdated attitudes regarding the amateurism of volunteers by being as professional as possible in all volunteering activities.

It is worth remembering that many volunteers are highly qualified, skilled and experienced and hold or have previously held positions of rank and responsibility.

Volunteering is not about sacrifice or being a martyr.

When people care about something to which they are volunteering, they might find themselves devoting more time to that than they had originally intended. This may be because there aren't enough people to complete necessary tasks; the volunteers involved may not be very good at saying no; their good nature, willingness and commitment might be being taken advantage of. These factors can lead to burnout in volunteers, which is not healthy for them or for the project in which they are involved.

There are some jobs in community situations that are not very interesting or stimulating; that might be uncomfortable or even unpleasant, yet need to be done by somebody. Those asked to carry out the work do not always have to be the same people. Even though difficult or tiresome jobs can be humbling and can be useful for keeping the ego in check, I would have some concern about a person who consistently volunteers for unpleasant, extremely challenging or tedious work, when there are others who could take their turn with these tasks. I have observed that when these types of jobs are rotated within the community this can offer many people the opportunity to develop humility and perhaps compassion for those less fortunate than themselves.

> It is important to have strategies in place for finding, recruiting, supporting, managing, empowering and keeping volunteers.

There can be any number of reasons why people would choose a particular community, project, group or organization with whom to volunteer. It is up to those groups and communities to make themselves and their work as attractive to these volunteers as possible, and, after recruiting them, to support them to be effective and to help them to find enjoyment and fulfillment through that volunteering.

> In my experience, the most effective way of achieving this is through those volunteers feeling empowered in all of their volunteering activities.

Anyone who has some responsibility for managing, directing or supporting volunteers would be wise to develop their skills for supporting the empowerment of those volunteers.

There is a belief that empowerment is not something that one person can provide for or develop in another and that empowerment is something that has to be self-generated in and by each individual. While this may be the case, there are unquestionably attitudes and behaviors that we can each develop that will support the self-empowerment of other people; just as there are attitudes and behaviors that we can suppress in ourselves to prevent these from undermining other people.

Appreciating and respecting volunteers

There can be some misconceptions and assumptions made in community situations where volunteering takes place. I have observed groups, organizations and communities where people believe there to be an unending supply of volunteers who can take the place of any who leave their service. This assumption can lead to volunteers being taken for granted or treated without due care and respect. In some cases this results in those groups, organizations or communities getting a bad reputation among volunteers. This will be unfortunate in the coming years as the competition for volunteer help grows. Occasionally this attitude has resulted in the failure of community projects.

I have occasionally observed a tendency by some full time residents of communities to look down on volunteers who they believe to be less committed to the community and its purpose than they are themselves. Volunteers have even been considered by some of these residents to somehow deserve less respect from them than do their fellow residents.

This attitude is surprisingly prevalent in some spiritual communities (modern or traditional) and in those dedicated to raising environmental awareness through their way of living and working. Some residents in these types of communities have been known to believe that their years of spiritual practice or their huge commitment to their work or to the environment makes them members of some kind of elite group. The sense of self-importance that can result from this belief might lead them to be demeaning towards volunteers and to assume a right to receive volunteer support. While these attitudes are rare within local communities, there are still people whose significant commitment to a community's development and sustainability, even in a voluntary capacity, allows them to feel some sense of superiority over volunteers whose commitment and involvement they consider to be less significant than their own.

It is important to remember that people will be involved in their volunteer activities through choice. They will be giving their time freely. They will be offering their skills, expertise and experience because they want to make a contribution. Without volunteers many communities and initiatives might not get off the ground. If they do, they may not function well or fully achieve their purpose. In some cases, they might not continue to exist.

> Regardless of their reasons for volunteering, volunteers ought to be highly respected and deeply appreciated.

The book, EMPOWERING VOLUNTEER MANAGEMENT, contains strategies for recruiting volunteers; empowering and supporting them to reach high standards of excellence in their volunteering; and ways to show appreciation for their time and efforts that will help them to feel fulfilled through their volunteer work. This is available from Amazon in paperback and e-book formats and accessible through our website: www.youmakethedifference.net

When people are willing to offer some of their time, skill and experience to improve those things that affect their lives and the lives of those around them they could be making a significant positive difference to their community. To do this through participating in groups and becoming involved in community projects is simple, empowering, mutually supportive, and it can be a lot of fun!

Advisors

It could be beneficial to engage with other supportive people who offer some necessary specialist skills and experience. Many people would love an opportunity to make a difference to a community initiative that inspires them - seek them out and invite them to share their knowledge and skills and be part of your exciting venture.

Some specialist information or experience needed for community sustainability might not be available within the community membership - seek advice from elsewhere. Perhaps some people who do not have an inclination to be community members would be prepared to be part of an advisory group.

> There is a lot of wisdom and experience going to waste out there.

Through voluntary or enforced retirement, redundancy or unemployment there are many people with valuable knowledge, skills and experience who might be no longer in a position to use them. These people, especially retirees, may not want to find replacement employment or to spend a lot of their newly acquired leisure time in a working environment. However, they may be willing to spend a small amount of time offering their knowledge and experience in an advisory capacity.

> Experts can advise on almost on any subject: financial systems; management strategies; IT systems, interpersonal communications; people and group management; meeting methods; dealing with statutory bodies and the media and many more areas that could be beneficial to fledgling communities and initiatives.

An advisory panel can provide much of the expertise required. This can also do away with the need to set up the management of the community or initiative along hierarchical lines in order to have experts involved at a top level. Instead, advisers can support the community to be managed co-operatively within a flatter structure: one in which a greater number of those in the community participate in its management and decision-making processes.

Put the word out and ask around. People working in the Voluntary and community Sector, in businesses or government agencies may know of people within them or former colleagues now retired or moved who might be willing and interested in voluntarily advising your community.

Using Advisors

Many intentional communities and voluntary community initiatives are created and managed by caring people. These are often the kind of people who don't like to upset others, who try to make everything nice for everyone, who want to work in a relaxed, harmonious, companionable and cooperative environment and who prefer to avoid making tough decisions; decisions that are likely to be unpopular with some people. Whilst these attitudes have many advantages they can also create problems. They can lead to inefficiency, ineffectiveness, frustration and possibly non-sustainability!

Advice offered on how to do things differently, to alleviate some of these problems is obviously likely to include developing attitudes, making decisions and taking actions that are opposite to the ones that have created any current problems. This can lead to resistance by people in the community to acting upon the advice given by those from outside the community - regardless of how professional or experienced those people may be. This could be because some people within the community feel embarrassed at having their faults or failures identified. Some might feel reluctant to implement procedures and processes with which they are unfamiliar or that they consider to be alien to the community culture.

As even inefficient or ineffective people will have probably been doing the very best they could do, it would be sensible, and kind, to acknowledge and appreciate their efforts and to introduce the advised new or revised procedures to them in a manner they would find easily acceptable.

Making the most of advisors
    a. Be clear about what kind of advice you need.
    b. Become aware of what kind of advice is on offer.
    c. Provide your advisers with all the information they need upon which to base their advice.
    d. Have advisers liaise with the appropriate people in your community.
    e. Have everyone or representatives of everyone who will be affected by any advised changes present at their presentations.
    f. Create opportunities for those people to have discussions and to offer ideas and suggestions for how these advised changes could be best implemented.

Be open-minded
Not all advice will be applicable and some might not be very palatable.

> However, there is no point in seeking advice if you do not intend to follow at least some of that advice.

I have observed a number of occasions where communities have sought advice from experts and then rejected that advice because it did not fit the culture of that community. 'We don't do that sort of thing', 'that's not who we are', 'that won't work here', are phrases that I heard expressed to well-intentioned people offering advice based upon years of experience.

Rejecting or accepting advice

Rejecting

> It will be wise to resist any temptation to reject advice out of hand.

Refusing to consider making the advised changes will probably result in business as usual, which might not only result in your community's problems remaining, it could also gain you a reputation for inflexibility and unwillingness to be advised.

You also have some responsibility towards the person whose advice you have sought. I have witnessed well-intentioned experts feeling disrespected when the advice they carefully gave was ignored or rejected. As a result of this, other experts were not so willing to offer advice in the future.

If, for whatever reason, the advice sought is not going to be taken then this ought to be communicated respectfully to the advisor. He or she deserves a full explanation of the reasons for rejecting their advice and ought to be appropriately appreciated for their efforts to be supportive and for the information and precious time they have given.

Accepting
Implementing advised changes might be difficult for some people in the community and could lead them to feel disappointed or frustrated in being unable to continue in their preferred manner. They may feel their past well-meaning approaches have not been successful, appreciated, valued or properly understood. Implementing advice to radically change attitudes and working practices might result in discontentment or resentment within the community - especially if the people affected do not understand why those changes are necessary or refuse to acknowledge that they do.

Finding a middle way

There is usually a middle way to be found in most situations. Even if the adviser does not understand the culture of your community or the reasons behind the development of that culture they are still likely to have offered some suggestions that could sensibly be taken.

Options:

- a. Advice sought from experts ought to be carefully considered.
- b. Look for bits of the advice that could be taken.
- c. Implement any advised changes in small incremental steps whenever possible.
- d. Bring everyone involved on board in making these changes.
- e. Explain what these changes are, why they are necessary and what they are intended to achieve.
- f. Seek ideas and suggestions from those to be affected by the changes on how these would be best implemented.
- g. Monitor progress and have simple feedback systems in place.
- h. Keep your advisors updated with the progress and results of their input.

Individuals and communities rarely seek advice when things are going well. Advice is usually sought only when things are going badly or when people don't know what they can do to improve some situation or to prevent some potential calamity. This might be described as 'fire-fighting'.

Remember: To prevent the 'fires' from starting it could be wise to use periods of calm to assess situations and needs and to create strategies.

5

GOVERNANCE: LEGAL AND
MANAGEMENT STRUCTURES

Whether forming an intentional community, or setting up a community initiative, there are several legal and organizational structures to choose from. These include: Unincorporated Associations, Trusts, Limited Companies, Charitable Incorporated Organizations, Co-operatives, Industrial and Provident Societies, Community Benefit Societies and Community Interest Companies. A search online will provide information on all of these.

Social Enterprise

A fairly recently devised structure that could be beneficial to local initiatives, and some intentional communities too, is that of Social Enterprise. The main benefit in developing a Social Enterprise is the greater autonomy it provides to a community project. In being able to create income a Social Enterprise is less dependent upon traditional forms of fundraising.

It seems to me that in the foreseeable future, Grants are going to be harder to find and available funding from traditional sources is going to be sought after by increasing numbers of potentially desperate organizations.

> Being able to generate some income allows a Social Enterprise to be self-determining to some extent and to utilize supportive and ethical business models.

Some intentional communities and community enterprises have goods to sell, the profits from which support the community, local, social activities or provide some benefit to others. Some offer services - sometimes, essential services - for which they can be remunerated.

> Whatever form a Social Enterprise takes, it is imperative that the intention is to be of **social benefit**. This is what distinguishes a Social Enterprise from a business that is run only to create profit for its owners, shareholders or investors. YOU MAKE THE DIFFERENCE is a Social Enterprise.

There is an excellent description of A Voluntary Code of Practice for Social Enterprise to download from Social Enterprise Scotland that clears up any confusion about what constitutes a Social Enterprise. This Code of Practice lays an inspiring and firm foundation of values, ethics, practices and behavior for Social Enterprises to follow: www.senscot.org

Transition Enterprise

These are a variation on Social Enterprises that have evolved out of the Transition Town Movement.

Along with community sustainability these usually operate with a high level of environmental awareness.

The following is the description from the Transition network website:

Characteristics of a Transition Enterprise

1. Resilience outcome – *TEs contribute to the increased resilience of communities in the face of, for example, economic uncertainty, energy and resource shortages and climate change impacts. As part of their community, TEs are also resilient in themselves, seeking to be financially sustainable and as independent as possible of external funding.*
2. Appropriate resource use - *TEs make efficient and appropriate use of natural resources (including energy), respecting finite limits and minimizing and integrating waste*

streams. The use of fossil fuels in particular is minimized.

3. Appropriate localization – *TEs operate at a scale appropriate to the environment, economy and business sector with regard to sourcing, distribution and interaction with the wider economy.*

4. More than profit – *TEs exist to provide affordable, sustainable products and services and decent livelihoods rather than to generate profits for others. TEs can be profitable, but the use of their excess profits prioritizes the community benefit rather than benefit to investors.*

5. Part of the community - *TEs work towards building a common wealth, owned and controlled as much as is practical by their workers, customers, users, tenants and communities. They have structures or business models, which are as open, autonomous, equitable, democratic, inclusive and accountable as possible. They complement and work in harmony with other TEs.*

Legal entities

Many people switch off in conversations about legal structures. Yet the legal structure of a group affects its behavior and how others see it. Flexibility and informality is fine for a young initiative, but as you grow and take on more responsibilities you will need more structure and allocation of responsibility.

No single approach fits every Transition group. You have to decide what is right for you, depending on what you are doing or planning, what sources of funding you intend to apply to and how well the group can handle administration such as minute keeping and filing returns. You also need to consider how more formality will affect the group (for example, some people are unfamiliar with and suspicious of formal structures and may feel excluded by too formal an approach).

You may eventually need more than one entity. If you decide to set up a business, for example, you will have to create an independent organization (probably a Community Interest Company or a Cooperative to own it). The structure does not have to be permanent – you can change your legal form to match your circumstances. Doing so is time consuming and can be expensive, but there is no need to be trapped in an unsuitable structure.

You must decide whether to apply to register as a charity. The aims of most Transition groups will qualify as charitable. Registering as a charity makes fundraising easier. However, the registration process is slow and can be tricky for those unfamiliar with the procedures. Once established, you must make sure you comply with charity law and the rules set out by the Charity Commission.

For many groups, the right initial choice will be to form a club (or 'unincorporated association', to give it its full legal name). This is easy to set up (a simple constitution must be drawn up and signed) and has minimal ongoing formality or administration. Provided the club's income is less than £1,000 per year, you don't have to register as a charity. Clubs need a written constitution that is formally adopted by the group.

Sample constitutions of Transition groups

These can be found online, and you can copy one and adapt it for your needs. Some groups may be happy to remain a club; others may decide to become a limited company – a step up in complexity and administration. This should be quite straightforward – conversion from a club to a company is hardly more complicated than forming a new company.

You should view choosing and forming a legal structure as an opportunity to clarify the group's vision and aims. The legal structure should not be chosen by a small clique and imposed on the group. It is far better to arrange for proper discussion about the options, to allow the parts of your group to have their say.

Download sample constitutions and see more at:
http://www.transitionnetwork.org/about.

This website also offers very useful information on many topics of interest to community groups and projects such as helpful material on insurance:

Governance and management structures

In deciding upon a governance or management structure there are a variety from which to choose.

Within the world of business there is a recognition that managerial structures are flattening out. However, surprisingly, many groups and organizations in the Community Sector are often still set up with hierarchical structures such as a Board of Trustees, a board of Directors or a management committee. This means that a handful of people, either self-appointed or elected by a membership, have a large measure of or even total control over most of the decisions made. Many of the people in these positions are wise, altruistic and take their responsibilities seriously. Unfortunately, sometimes, the people in these positions have personal agendas. Some carry out their duties either less than effectively or without due care and attention to how their decisions affect others involved within the community or organization.

The pitfalls of this type of hierarchical structure are often exacerbated by the mix of volunteers and paid employees. Employees and volunteers can have different requirements and reasons for their involvement. They might also have different criteria for making decisions and have different ways of measuring success.

My book, EMPOWERING VOLUNTEER MANAGEMENT, explores how volunteers in groups and organizations can and ought to be supported by those in managerial positions. The other side of the same coin is how voluntary committees, boards of trustees or directors can best support paid employees.

I have observed and experienced occasions when voluntary boards or committees have made decisions that have not taken into account the advice from, or the well-being of, paid employees. Also times when necessary actions have not been taken by them to guarantee those employees the resources or support they have needed to carry out their work.

If such hierarchical structures are to be continued with there will be a requirement for greater transparency and the implementation of improved systems of checks, balances and accountability of board and committee members. I believe that in the Community Sector there will be an increased demand for greater transparency, more inclusivity and wider representation in management and decision-making. Wise people are creating or restructuring community groups and organizations with structures to accomplish these.

The following are ways in which transparency and accountability can be achieved:

a. Have representatives from all areas and stakeholder groups involved in decision-making.
b. Create overlapping circles of information and responsibility.
c. Have regular consultations with all those involved.
d. Have managerial discussion and decisions observed by some or all of those involved in the community or project.

Remember: Seeking opinions from members, workers and volunteers as well as having an advisory board of skilled and experienced people will widen the available pool of information, experience and expertise.

Sociocracy

> The Sociocratic model of governance, management and decision-making is fast becoming a method favored among many intentional communities, especially Ecovillages and CoHousing projects. I believe it could also well serve Transition Towns and other community-led initiatives.

The Wikipedia website provides an interesting historical perspective and detailed descriptions of Sociocracy that includes the following information:

Sociocracy is English for the word Sociocratie, coined in 1851 by August Comte and was later used by the U.S. sociologist Lester Frank Ward and later still by Dutchman

Kees Boeke. Boeke saw Sociocracy as a form of governance that presumes equality of individuals and is based on consent. This equality is not expressed with the "one man, one vote" law of democracy but rather by a group of individuals reasoning together until a decision is reached. In the 1970s, Gerard Endenburg, a former student of Boeke, further developed Boeke's three original principles and added the forth.

The Four Key Design Principles
1. *Decision Making on Policy Issues by Consent*
2. *Organizing in Circles*
3. *Double Linking*
4. *Elections by Consent*

Consent
Consent as defined and practiced in Sociocratic organizations is claimed to be a more efficient and effective decision-making method than autocratic decision-making, because it builds trust and understanding (Described later in the section on decision making).

Essential Principles

Consent Governs Policy Decision Making
Sociocracy makes a distinction between "consent" and "consensus."

Organizing in Circles
The Sociocratic organization is composed of a hierarchy of semi-autonomous circles. This hierarchy, however, does not constitute a power structure as autocratic hierarchies do. Each circle has the responsibility to execute, measure, and control its own processes in achieving its goals. It governs a specific domain of responsibility within the policies of the larger community or organization. Circles are also responsible for their own development and for each member's development. Often called "integral education" the circle and its members are expected to determine what they need to know to reach the goals of their circle.

Double-Linking
These links function as full members in the decision-making of both their own circles and the next higher circle, the General Management Circle. Operational leaders are selected by the next higher circle and represent the larger community or organization in the decision-making of the circles they lead. Representatives are selected by the circles to represent the circles interests in the next higher circle. These links form a feedback loop between circles.

At the highest level of the community or organization, there is a "top circle", similar to a Board of Directors, that connects the organization to its environment. Typically these members include representatives with expertise in such things as law and finance and the community or organization's mission. The top circle also includes the person holding the overall executive or leadership role and at least one representative of the general management circle. Each of these circle members participates fully in decision-making in the top circle.

Elections by Consent

Individuals are elected to roles and responsibilities in open discussion using the same consent criteria used for other policy decisions. Members of the circle nominate themselves or other members of the circle and present reasons for their choice. After discussion, people can (and often do) change their nominations, and the discussion leader will suggest the election of the person for whom there are the strongest arguments. Circle members may object and there is further discussion. For a role that many people might fill, this discussion may continue for a several rounds. When fewer people are qualified for the task, this process is short. The circle may also decide to choose someone who is not a current member of the circle.

Interdependence and Transparency

The principles are interdependent and the application of all of them is required for a community or organization to function Sociocratically. Each one supports the successful application of the others. The principles also require transparency in the community or organization. Since decision-making is distributed throughout the organization, all members of the organization must have access to information. The only exception to this is proprietary knowledge and any information that would jeopardize the security of the community or organization or those they serve. All financial transactions and policy decisions are transparent to members of the community or organization.

In addition to the principles, Sociocratic organizations apply the circular feedback process of directing-doing-measuring to the design of work and community processes.

Inclusiveness

For communities and organizations accustomed to consensus decision-making, what sociocracy brings to governance is a governance structure that is based on the consensus decision-making process. It uses a structured consensus, or delegated overlapping consensus. Consent of Circle A can be maintained in Circle B without all the members of Circle A participating because Circle A and Circle B overlap. Equally important is that the ways in which they overlap have the consent of both circles.

Because inclusiveness in everyday community life requires consensus, consensus becomes a practice, not just in formal decision-making process restricted to meetings.

"Everything depends on a new spirit breaking through among men. May it be that, after the many centuries of fear, suspicion and hate, more and more a spirit of reconciliation and mutual trust will spread abroad. The constant practice of the art of sociocracy and of the education necessary for it seem to be the best way in which to further this spirit, upon which the real solution of all world problems depends." Kees Boeke

More useful information on Sociocracy can be found by searching the web.

Making decisions

The way in which decisions are made is a significant factor in any community's culture.

In the making of major decisions within small communities and groups it ought to be possible for all of the members involved to take part. In larger communities and initiatives some sort of steering or core group will traditionally probably take most major decisions; although, this is now changing with the adoption of new systems of decision-making.

In democratic intentional communities and local community governance a council of some description will usually make decisions affecting the community. However, decisions that will have an impact on the people within the community ought to be made only after consultation or some level of engagement with everyone concerned. This can prevent a few people feeling resentful about having to implement or live with decisions that have been taken without their involvement.

> Having resentful and disempowered people in an organization is bad enough; when this happens within community it is a recipe for disaster.

People are much more likely to want to make any decision work if they have had a hand in making it. The people 'on the ground' as it were, are also more likely to be the ones with the most experience and information about the matter under discussion. To ignore this would seem to be a waste of a valuable source of information.

To give people some autonomy and control within any community, the small or day-to-day decisions would best be delegated to those people who have the responsibility for carrying them out - sociocratic circles of decision making would seem to be appropriate for this.

Having a chain of command for the making of little everyday decisions within a community is usually unnecessarily cumbersome and inefficient and might slow down progress and speed up disempowerment and resentment.

Majority vote

The method most commonly used for arriving at a decision is through a majority vote, where it will first be necessary to establish what percentage of those present constitutes the majority. This may vary from 60% to 90%, although around 75% is most common. In my experience this is an occasion where the 80/20 rule can be usefully employed, as 80% clearly is the majority. Determining 80% of those present is an easy calculation.

A loyal minority

When a decision is reached by a majority of people, there is sometimes a tendency amongst the remaining minority to be disgruntled about the decision and to be disruptive in some way. This can be anything from persistent grumbling about the decision to actively attempting to undermine it. To avoid this, an important part of the majority voting process is to request those who are in disagreement with the decision to be recognized as a loyal minority.

These people ought to have been given ample opportunity to express their opinion before the vote was taken and so everyone present can be aware of their concerns. After the decision is made these concerns can be acknowledged by the meeting manager with a request for a commitment from those people to be loyal to the group by resisting any temptation to chip away at the decision through criticism or negative judgments or to desist from any action that could undermine the implementation of the decision. Each of these participants ought to be encouraged to make this commitment verbally. They ought then to be appreciated for their willingness to be supportive of the majority choice.

If those people fail to keep to their commitment at any time during the period the decision is being implemented they could be reminded of their commitment to be loyal to the group. If, at some stage in the future, the concerns of this minority prove to be accurate, then their foresight ought to be acknowledged and appreciated.

Reaching Consensus

The ideal method for a group to reach a decision is through consensus.

Full consensus is achieved when everyone present agrees upon a decision. In order to reach this point work may need to be done on clarifying and refining the proposal. Sub issues or different facets of the topic can muddy the waters and bog down process. Dealing with these effectively is vital to consensus.

To reach consensus there are a number of things to bear in mind:

a. The more contentious the issue the more difficult it usually is to reach consensus.

b. The greater the number of people involved in the decision the more difficult it is likely to be to reach consensus.

c. Reaching full consensus can be a lengthy process requiring patience, commitment and clear, honest communication from everyone involved.

d. The greater the number of people involved in the decision the longer it is likely to take to reach consensus.

e. Arriving at consensus on an important or contentious issue might take several meetings. If any of the factors in these meetings are changed, such as people leaving the process or new people coming into it, the process is likely to be prolonged.

Reaching consensus

There are variations on the process of consensus. Here is one:

Phase 1

The issue upon which consensus is to be achieved needs to be clearly stated.

Phase 2

Those of differing opinions gather into groups of like-minded people. For example those who would intend to vote 'yes' collect into one group, those who would vote 'no' gather into another and those who are undecided gather into a third group.

Phase 3

Each group comes up with clear statements of their reasons for their opinion and chooses one, or in the case of large groups two, representatives to make these.

Phase 4

These representatives meet in the centre of the room where they are facilitated, in full view of everyone, to put forward their group's views and opinions about the topic and the reasons for their group's current decision.

Phase 5

The representatives then return to their groups, which discuss whether or not what they have heard from other groups has influenced their group's current decision. It is possible that having a clearer understanding of other people's perspectives, a consensus decision can be reached at this point. If not, each group discusses what they have heard and then comes up with a proposal that could help a move towards consensus. For example the 'no' or 'don't know' group might come up with a statement - something like: 'we could move closer to agreement if...' they state their new proposal. The 'yes' group could make a proposal that accommodates some of the wishes or concerns of the other two groups.

Phase 6

The representatives return to the centre of the room and offer their group's proposals or new thinking. They then go back to their groups where the new proposals and ideas heard from the other groups are considered. It is possible that consensus may be reached at this point if concerns or requests have been accommodated satisfactorily.

This process continues with the representatives going backwards and forwards to communicate their group's evolving thinking or their suggested adjustments to the proposal. Consensus is reached when everyone in the room can agree. This method of reaching consensus usually requires some compromise to be made by each group.

Large groups might have their discussions in separate rooms with only their representatives having a full sense of the overall picture. However, this can add to the existing feelings of separation created by the differing opinions and is likely to prevent the meeting from being fully inclusive. When all of the groups occupy areas of the same room for their discussions and can observe the representative's exchanges this allows the whole of the process to be transparent and to create a sense of 'we are all in this together'.

A last resort

To reach a necessary or urgent decision within a time scale, an agreement could already have been made to switch to majority voting as a last resort if consensus cannot be achieved within the allocated time. In these circumstances it is especially important to fully recognize the concerns of those unwilling to agree to consensus and to establish them as a committed Loyal Minority Group for which they ought to be acknowledged.

Consent

Consent is fundamental to Socratic decision-making.

Sociocracy makes a distinction between "consent" and "consensus." Consent is defined in Sociocracy as "no objections," and objections are based on one's ability to work toward the aims of the organization. While neither consent nor consensus is usually practiced as requiring unanimous agreement, traditionally consensus is often confused with both unanimous agreement and the exercise of personal values. Consensus is most often practiced as a full-group decision-making and not distributed decision-making. In Sociocracy, consent is defined and practiced in conjunction with the other principles and can support a complex organizational structure.

Decisions are made when there are no remaining "paramount objections", that is, when there is informed consent from all participants. Objections must be reasoned and argued and based on the ability of the objector to work productively toward the goals of the community or organization. All policy decisions are made by consent although the group may by consent decide to use another decision-making method. Within these policies, day-to-day operational decisions are normally made in the traditional manner.

Consent as defined and practiced in Sociocratic organizations is claimed to be a more efficient and effective decision-making method than autocratic decision-making, because it builds trust and understanding. The process educates the participants about the needs of the other members in doing their work effectively as well as their psychological and social needs as human beings. In addition to reducing friction, the well-defined, information-based, and highly disciplined process helps a group stay focused and move swiftly through examining an issue and actual decision-making.

"Only when common agreement is reached can any action be taken, quite a different atmosphere is created from that arising from majority rule."
Kees Boeke

He defined three "fundamental rules": (1) That the interests of all members must be considered and the individual must respect the interests of the whole. (2) No action could be taken without solutions that everyone could accept, and (3) all members must accept these decisions when unanimously made. If a group could not make a decision it would be made by a "higher level" of representatives chosen by each group. The size of a decision-making group should be limited to 40 with smaller committees of 5-6 making "detailed decisions." For larger groups a structure of representatives are chosen by these groups to make decisions.

One step further

There is a further step that can be taken towards reaching consensus that was demonstrated in a consensus decision-making training run by my friend Robin Shohet.

We trainees were invited to pair up with someone of around an equal size to ourselves. We were then asked to arm wrestle with each other. As expected, the strongest of each pair won.

We were then asked to each think of an ideal outcome to some personal or global difficulty and to share that with our wrestling partner. We were to imagine that whoever in the pair won the next bout of arm wrestling could magically achieve their desired outcome. Even though we each passionately pleaded our cause to our opponents, in the hope of eliciting their understanding and support, in most cases, although not all, the strongest person in each pair won again.

Robin then prepared to arm wrestle one of the participants. Robin's ideal outcome was world peace and the participant's was the eradication of global poverty. The winner of this seemed to be a foregone conclusion as one man was two meters tall and strongly built, while the other was of much shorter and lighter stature. The bout took only two seconds. Each of them released the others hand and they both place their arms in their 'winning' positions. It was immediately clear that this had been prearranged and that both men were attempting to allow the other to succeed!

Robin then explained that he had approached the arm wrestling bout with the intention of wanting the participant to achieve his desired outcome. The participant explained that he had had the same intention regarding Robin.

Of course, this was so obvious. Why would the participant not want Robin to achieve his ideal of world peace? Why would Robin not want this person to have his ideal outcome of the eradication of poverty? This only required a small shift from 'how can I stop you getting what you want' to 'how can I help you to get what you want.' From 'one of us has to lose for the other to win' to 'how can we help each other to get our needs met?' This was all so simple! And yet it changed everything!

This simple shift of intention from needing to win to wanting to find an agreement where others also achieve their goals or fulfill their needs expands thinking, frees up creativity and engages our compassion and commitment to doing the right thing.

> This is a small step of changing intention, which can be a giant leap in community decision-making.

When hearing this process described, some people say, 'Yes but, this doesn't make any sense, nobody wins!'

On the contrary, if my intention is for you to achieve your goals and I have done whatever I can to bring that about, I will gain a sense of accomplishment. So will you, if you have done the same for me. This is Win-Win!

Another statement that is sometimes made about this process is, 'What if two groups of people want totally opposite results or for one group to get what they want means that it is detrimental to the other group?' In my experience, most situations within communities are rarely so polarized.

This process is similar to some that are used to deal with serious conflict. If this process can be successfully employed to resolve life threatening conflict situations around the world, it can surely be helpful within group, organizational or community situations. I have not yet experienced any everyday situation that could not be resolved to the sufficient satisfaction of two seemingly opposing needs. There is usually enough common ground or mutual aim that can be built upon to reach a workable solution, even if that might require continuous monitoring.

Another concern expressed is 'Yes but what if I behave generously and make a decision to help others to get what they want and then they don't do the same for me?'

My usual reply is, so what? What was your real intention? Did you genuinely intend for that person to get what they needed? If so that ought not to be affected by anything that happens to you. You made your choice and they made theirs.

> Just because somebody might not behave in the manner that we would like, that ought not to prevent us from behaving in the way that we believe to be right.

> We each face choices, small and large, every minute of the day. Many of these choices are whether to be part of a problem or part of a solution. For we human beings to create a society and to evolve into a species of mutually supportive, compassionate people, requires us to choose to be part of the solutions rather than part of the problems.

We can all choose to do the very best that we can in this regard at any given time.

Making a Quantum leap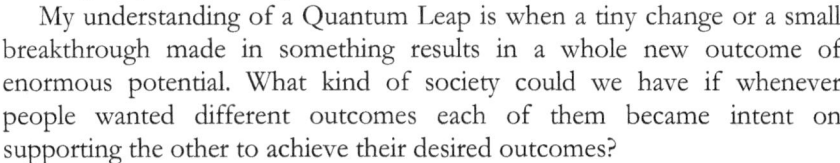

My understanding of a Quantum Leap is when a tiny change or a small breakthrough made in something results in a whole new outcome of enormous potential. What kind of society could we have if whenever people wanted different outcomes each of them became intent on supporting the other to achieve their desired outcomes?

What changes in our attitudes, our thinking and our decision-making would be required when we want those with whom we are in discussion or disagreement to get what they need?

Would it require us to have greater understanding of people? Would it require us to see past our own needs to the needs of others and the reason for their desired outcomes? Would this require us to see people as having value equal to that of our own?

> Perhaps this small change in each of us in the focus of our attention from 'me' to 'we' is all that is needed to make the Paradigm Shift from a world in which we compete with one another for everything into a world of genuine cooperation towards Global sustainability?

There are several useful processes for decision making in the books: ENJOYABLE & EFFECTIVE MEETINGS and EFFORTLESS FACILITATION in this series, available from Amazon and accessible through: www.youmakethedifference.net

The role of Listener Convener

Many intentional communities have spent years experimenting with systems, structures, and methods of management that would include and best support the residents and members. Cooperative structures that sustain democratic systems, some forms of community councils, full consultations and inclusive decision-making are obviously beneficial as is transparency of information and discussions.

One method for achieving transparency of information was first devised in the Tui Community in New Zealand and further developed by the New Findhorn (Community) Association in Scotland. This method was for the election of Listener Conveners.

The role of Listener Convener in the Findhorn Community

The role of Listener Convener is to be the ears of the Community. To be the person who:
1. Takes the pulse of the community.
2. Listens to the concerns, ideas and suggestions of Community members.
3. Listens for conflicts between individuals or within organizations.
4. Listens to hear of innovative ideas.
5. Listens to spot trends and to observe the Community mood.
6. Welcomes new members.
7. Supports organizations and businesses.
8. Empower grassroots members to take new initiatives.
9. Facilitates communication across the Community.

After bringing what has been heard and observed to the attention of the Community Council for discussion and decision, a Listener Convener is to implement the decisions made by Council. He or she is to convene whatever meeting seems appropriate to share that information, address those concerns and support the ideas and suggestions that could help move the Community forward in its aims. These meetings might be brief discussions of a few interested people or gatherings of the whole Community to address issues that affect them all. They might be to raise awareness, to resolve conflict or to contribute towards the development of the Community.

The Listener Convener also initiates or supports the development of Community projects and activities.

The Community Members elect the Listener Convener to the post and pay his or her salary from their membership subscription.

The Listener Convener is to be available to; accountable to, and in support of the individual Community Members while keeping in mind the needs and aims of the Community as a whole and to hold an awareness of the way in which the Community is perceived.

Having held this post for four years during the time in which the Findhorn Community restructured itself I can attest to the many benefits that this role can offer a community.

Through Listener Conveners (LCs) there is a clear, unbiased conduit through which people can channel their ideas, concerns and questions to the appropriate people. This encourages greater openness of expression. As does knowing that these will not fall on 'deaf ears', be ignored or get lost in bureaucracy.

By having a grasp of what is going on within the community, LCs can provide relevant information to the people holding responsibility for specific aspects of the community; and ensure that all necessary information is available upon which decisions can be made. By being available to all community members and been given the authority to convene whatever meetings might be required to resolve difficulties or move ideas forward LCs can help reduce tension and conflict and ensure that creative thinking is not wasted.

The LCs chair and facilitate Council meetings in a non-voting capacity. As the role is one of neutrality an LC will sometimes need to set aside their personal opinions and preferences in order to effectively carry out their responsibilities for the benefit of the community as a whole.

Knowing that LCs are available to listen to them, individuals have no need to feel isolated or excluded. Knowing that LCs are available to observe their discussions and meetings enables organizations and groups within the community to hear how their thinking fits with the greater scheme of things. Having LCs represent the community when involved in group and organization discussions and decision-making gives the whole community a voice in these. Having LCs available to facilitate their meetings gives groups access to experienced facilitation.

By having elected LCs as representatives who have a wide understanding of the community, and are available to participate in local and regional discussions and events gives a community a voice in exploring and deciding upon issues in the district and region.

> From my experience, I believe that the Listener Convener role is one that would be useful in most intentional communities and in many local communities also, particularly those that are going through regeneration and/or becoming transition towns.

Having one person, or two part-time people, being available to receive and to disseminate information could be very helpful to any community, especially during times change.

Skills and attributes

> Obviously a Listener Convener would need to have good listening skills.

Meeting management and facilitation skills would also be beneficial, as would an understanding of group dynamics and community development. Other useful attributes would be the ability to see the big picture while paying attention to some of the important details; patience with, compassion and respect for other people, high integrity and a strong commitment to the community.

6

LEADERSHIP

In any community or initiative there may be an obvious leader. This might be, and often is, the person who started it. In some instances there may be no obvious leader, although there might be a need for one - at least for a while at the beginning.

What makes a good leader?

I have asked this question of hundreds of people. Their replies indicate that there are many opinions on the subject:

1. People who are inspirational.
2. People with vision.
3. People with the ideas.
4. People with the drive and enthusiasm to get those ideas off the ground.
5. People with the strategies for success.
6. People with the expertise and experience to make those strategies become reality.
7. People with charisma.
8. People who instill confidence.
9. People who understand how to motivate and get the best out of others.
10. People who encourage others by their sheer hard work or dogged determination.

> Although I have met some exceptionally gifted leaders, it is unrealistic to expect all of these qualities to be combined in one individual.

We often have high, sometimes unrealistic, expectations of people in leadership roles, which, in my experience, they are almost certain to fail to reach at some time or another. The higher our expectations of leaders, the greater our disappointment in them is likely to be if they fail to meet them. The resulting feelings of disempowerment of the leaders and the disillusionment of the people being led can be painful for all concerned, and may have disastrous consequences for a community.

Communities provide many opportunities for people to explore many aspects of leadership. Having an understanding of what leadership means and how best to manage leadership roles within a community can be empowering for individuals. This understanding might make the difference to the success of a community or whether or not it remains sustainable.

Leadership Myths

There are a number of myths surrounding leadership. As with many myths these might have become a way of explaining things. They may have become part of some people's belief system. For others, these myths can be useful for keeping the status quo. Some investigation of these myths could prove useful when considering leadership roles within communities.

Myth #1, Leader is another word for 'Boss'

The word leader can bring up a lot of emotions in people. To some people the word 'leader' represents power or authority. These might be what some people want, some people shy away from having and some people resent in those who have them.

Unfortunate attitudes have developed as a result of how the power of leadership has been used and abused in the past. One of these is the belief that anyone who is egotistical enough to want to be a leader is obviously too egotistical to be trusted with the role!

I believe that this attitude towards leadership has no place in most communities and it would be wise for the people in them to dispel the myth that leader means boss in their community.

Myth #2, Leaders are born not made

Belief in this myth has allowed people, perceived to be born to lead, to assume leadership roles - whether they are suitable for them or not. Just because a person has some status in society, has been well educated, has been successful in business or the military, or has led some form of campaign does not automatically make them the most appropriate leaders in communities.

This myth can also blind people to their own leadership potential or that of those around them. I have seen this belief prevent the most suitable leadership candidates from stepping forward, and the people within a community from recognizing the leadership potential of those people or having the willingness to be led by them.

> From experience it seems to me that natural leaders emerge naturally.

The natural leader for any situation will clearly emerge if the conditions are right. Those conditions can be created in a community when there is:

a. Trust among the community members.
b. Constructive communication between them.
c. A recognition and appreciation of the skills and experience within the community.
d. The willingness of the appropriate people to take a leadership role.
e. For the others in the community to support them to do so.

Myth #3, Leaders need to be charismatic

It can be very useful for the initiator of a community or a project to have a charismatic personality. I know of hundreds of projects around the world that only exist because some individuals had the vision, the determination and persistence to initiate them and the charisma to inspire others to join in. Some of these projects are small and local: skateboard parks, animal shelters for example. Others are enormous and global: rainforest protection and regeneration, the feeding of countless starving people.

However, having a charismatic leader can be a double-edged sword. One edge is a leader's ability to initiate and drive a project; to inspire people and attract the resources needed to maintain it. Just by being who they are, some people have a natural ability to inspire people. Maybe it is their passion for a project, their concern and compassion for others that stirs people into action. Their commitment and dedication might be what encourages loyal support from many people.

The other edge of the sword is the level of dependency that a project can come to have upon that person, on their charisma and upon an assumption that other beneficial attributes also exist in that leader. When, along with a charismatic personality, a person has other necessary leadership qualities then a project is likely to benefit and have a great start. In most cases however, it would be wise for those involved in the project, especially the leader, to fully involve other people who have the skills and experience needed to sustain the project.

Charismatic leaders can sometimes be so closely associated with ideas and ideals that it can be difficult to separate one from the other. In many situations this might not matter much. However, if it is perceived that to question one is an automatic attack on the other - whichever way round - this can create problems. There are plenty of examples of this, notably in religious and political movements, past and present. It could be useful for people to have some awareness of this possibility, which might help to avoid charismatic leaders becoming dictators, to become indispensable or giving groundless credibility to insubstantial projects, ideas or ideals.

Myth #4, Leaders must be passionate

A passionate and highly motivated leader may be one whose passion for a project is based upon emotion. This emotion may come from some personal experience, such as the illness or the loss of a loved one. It may come from a drive to fight injustice or right a wrong. It may come from a desire to provide care and nurturing to the needy where none exists. It might come from a determination to influence greater sustainability at a local or planetary level.

This passion often sustains levels of energy and enthusiasm in the leader that no other member of the project can match. This might lead to some leaders developing resentment towards others and result in the disempowerment or a sense of inadequacy among the members of the community or group. It can also encourage the leaders to cut corners or take risks that might be unwise and unfair or reasonable to ask others to do.

Remember: An effective passionate leader is one who recognizes that it is unlikely that the other people involved will have the same drive to achieve success for the project as they have, and, who think no less of others because of it!

Myth #5, 'Too many Chiefs and not enough Indians'

This is an old saying in my culture, which, along with another 'Too many cooks spoil the broth', warn against having too many people being involved in making decisions. This myth might apply in communities where there is an absence of agreed decision-making procedures or where the roles within the community are not clearly defined.

> This myth supports the old Paradigm of leaders and followers. In this Paradigm, a leader, or a very small community of people, make the decisions or give instructions, which everyone else involved obeys or carries out. This might have merit in some situations, however this approach is unlikely to prove to be the best method for empowering people in communities.

Myth #6, There is no need for leadership in cooperative communities

This is quite a modern myth, although some traces might be found in some past religious, political and social experiments. To many people this seems to be more of a utopian ideal than a realistic objective. Even so, this ideal could be well worth considering as part of our conscious evolutionary process.

From observation and experience, it seems to me that there are a number of elements essential for enabling 'leaderless' cooperative communities to function well and be effective:

1. Understanding and agreement of the purpose and objectives of the community by everyone involved.
2. Commitment to these, outweighing any personal opinions or needs, by everyone in the community.
3. Thorough understanding of the function of each member, their commitment and dedication to that function and the full support of the other members of the community.
4. Constant attention to community cohesion and the development of the community culture.
5. Fully inclusive, consensus decision-making.
6. Allegiance by everyone involved to the decisions made by the community.
7. Willingness for regular review and reflection.
8. Full engagement in any required improvement or transformation processes.

For all of these elements to be in place would require a community made up of quite enlightened people. I have learned that very few of us are as enlightened as we imagine ourselves to be.

There have been communities that have had some degree of success in establishing these elements. Even so, they have discovered that a huge amount of attention needs to be given to community processing and many things can take a long time to achieve while doing so. This can result in inadequate attention being paid to other important issues such as the wellbeing of the members, the improvement of technical skills and equipment needed to function in an ever-changing world and the acquiring and sensible management of resources.

With so much attention focused on internal processing, a leaderless community can become self-absorbed and less interested or effective in relating to people outside the community. The result can be elitism, a sense of superiority over people whose approaches are different or considered by the community to be inferior. This could be self-defeating to a community whose stated objectives are to be of service to others or to be an inspiration and a model of community.

I have noticed that much of the success of a seemingly leaderless community depends upon their reasons for being leaderless. In some communities, the reason has resulted from the community having experienced an authoritarian leader for a while and being determined to prevent any individual from having that level of power again. This has sometimes left these communities floundering around directionless for some time.

> Fear or suspicion of any form of leadership can itself become a form of tyranny, which disempowers people and prevents appropriate leaders from emerging.

Even so, in some communities the reason for wanting to be leaderless is a genuine desire for cooperative working and commitment to the mutual empowerment of all those involved. In these communities, each member will be encouraged by and will encourage and support fellow members to step into any leadership role whenever their skills and experience are what are needed.

Effective self-managing communities

> Communities provide the opportunity for people to turn this leaderless myth on its head. Rather than being a leaderless community, a community could be self-managing and made up of people taking leadership roles when appropriate or necessary.

Each of the members might embody one or more of the attributes of a good leader and so between them they would have all those aspects covered. The elements needed for an effective leaderless community, as previously described, would be essential; as would each member being committed to taking on the leadership role in his or her field of expertise and experience when required; and when each member of the community encourages and supports one another to do so.

This type of self-managing community might still feel the need for someone to hold the overall vision and to help members to keep aligned with it.

> It would be beneficial to have someone with facilitation skills to manage meetings and discussions, to coordinate communications among members and to disseminate information.

Within such a community there may be a requirement for people to coordinate teams. Some functions and activities of a community might need people with experience to direct operations. Whatever any of these functions are called in any community - these are leadership roles.

Leadership Styles

There are a variety of leadership styles, each having benefits and disadvantages and each being appropriate for particular situations. Some are more effective than others and it seems that a leadership style is often an extension of that leader's personality. These styles fall broadly into one of the following categories: authoritarian, democratic, facilitating.

Authoritarian Leadership

Authoritarian leaders lead from the top down and might be dictatorial towards their community members. They can be rigid in their thinking and may be difficult to deal with, especially when they are disagreed with.

There are other attributes that often come along with authoritarian leadership might hold a project back from reaching its full potential. These characteristics might include: pride, self-importance, self-righteousness and a sense of superiority. These can result in a number of situations:

a. The leader's unwillingness or inability to listen to the advice and ideas of others.

b. Their unwillingness to delegate functions and decision-making to others.

c. Their lack of patience and tolerance that might undermine or disempower community members, workers and volunteers.

d. Their inability to recognize their own lack of good communication skills.

e. Their inability to inspire good communications within the project or community.

f. Their unrealistically high assessment of their own skills and abilities.

g. Their low opinion of the skills and abilities of the other people involved.

Authoritarianism is sometimes confused with strong leadership, which, in my experience, it rarely is. In fact, any need a leader might have to be dictatorial, to get their own way or to bully people into submission could be based upon their insecurities along with their fear that these insecurities will be exposed. What is strong in that?

However, an authoritarian style of leadership - preferably without the negative attributes - might be vital in critical or dangerous situations where people need to be clearly guided or instructed in what to do. This style might be useful in the very early stages of getting a project off the ground.

Democratic Leadership

Democratic leaders are likely to delegate many of the leadership responsibilities to others in the community. They will work with those involved to set up systems and structures to empower the members. They will solicit proposals, encourage discussion, and include as many people as is feasible in decision-making. Within the community, the majority rules most of the time, although, this type of leader might occasionally exercise their veto during voting.

> Democratic leadership is most applicable for encouraging cooperation and creating a culture that will support positive community development.

Facilitating Leadership

Some leaders seem hardly to be leaders at all. They may choose to have very little control and formal influence upon most aspects of the community's activities, which they trust to be handled by the people who have taken responsibility for them. They facilitate community discussion and decision-making and are likely to choose to forego any power of veto.

Facilitating leadership is most suitable when a community has reached the cooperative stage in its development (described later) and those in the community have confidence and trust in themselves and in one another. Involvement from these leaders will then mostly be supportive and encouraging to members of the community as they carry out their tasks.

Each of these three styles will be suitable for specific circumstances.

Appropriate Leadership

> Appropriate leadership is just that - the appropriate style of leadership for the circumstances.

An appropriate leadership style is sometimes determined by timing. Getting a project off the ground may require some authoritarian leadership at the beginning. New projects, new organizations even new countries can benefit from a short period of benign authoritarian style of leadership. However, that is likely to only be effective for a while and will become unnecessary when co-operation and democratic decision-making are developed.

To develop community cohesion and cooperation, to build trust, to create openness and clear communication within a community will require a leadership style that is democratic, supportive and encouraging.

A self-managing community, functioning within a culture of cooperation and mutual respect, could then enjoy the benefits of a facilitating style of leadership.

The positive aspects of each of these styles can be implemented as needed or appropriate. For example:

1. When in charge of volunteers entering specific data into the computer a community or team leader might be authoritarian when instructing them how to carry out that task; there is no room for discussion, just a right and a wrong way to do it.

2. A leader might be democratic in discussions with their volunteer team on how to keep the phones manned over a period of time, such as the holiday season. He or she might explain what needs to happen and then discusses with them how this can be done to best suit everyone concerned. The team could then sort out a Rota or vote upon who will work the phones, and when. The team leader might veto an unrealistic plan; however, their intent would be to support whatever the team comes up with.

3. A leader might facilitate a community discussion about fundraising or ideas for new projects. In most cases it would be inappropriate for them to have more or less a say about these than anyone else in the community, especially those who have expertise. The appropriate members of the community would step up to take on the responsibility for implementing these ideas and projects. In this, as in many other situations, a facilitating leader would confidently trust their community colleagues to support one another in achieving the agreed aims.

It is occasionally possible for a person who has significant self-awareness and an understanding of community development to lead a community through all of the stages of its development. It seems to me that this is what Nelson Mandela managed to achieve in a country poised for civil war when he became leader; so this ought not to be impossible to achieve within an intentional community or a group intending to be helpful within its community!

Your choice

If you are the leader of a community, a team, a project or an activity, you may have already developed your leadership style or have a preference for one of them over the others. It might serve you and your community to consider if this choice is the most appropriate for the time and circumstances.

Some useful questions to consider:

a. Is this a conscious choice of leadership style or extension of your personality?

b. Is your choice of leadership style based on your needs or on the needs of the community?

c. What kind of leadership style might your project or community really need at this time?

d. Would your leadership style benefit from some flexible thinking?

A community being led along traditional lines might find it beneficial for the whole community to consider these questions regarding leadership. This is not intended to undermine any current leadership; it is to expand the community's awareness of leadership options.

> The key to choosing an appropriate leadership style for any situation is an awareness of the circumstances; the stage a community has reached in its development; sensitivity to the needs of the community; the characteristics of potential leaders and the flexibility to choose accordingly.

Being a leader

So far we've been concentrating upon the leadership roles of management and function. There are other aspects of leadership that impact the effectiveness and sustainability of any community or project. These aspects are about influencing the attitudes and behavior of fellow members and the culture of the community. This form of leadership is more about demonstrating cooperative and supportive ways of being and modeling the attitudes, behavior and methods of personal communication that inspires others and encourages community cohesion. It includes a willingness to take responsibility, not only for a function or an activity, also for one's thoughts, words and deeds and the consequences of any of these.

The seven C's of leadership

1. Commitment.
2. Creativity.
3. Communication.
4. Collaboration.
5. Co-operation.
6. Consensus.
7. Courage.

Commitment
Leadership and commitment go hand-in-hand. Leadership commitment means not only saying you that are committed to a principle, to a cause, to an outcome, to a way of doing things or to a community of people. It requires a demonstration of that commitment. If you are not seen to be committed to the cause, to the goals of the community, to the outcome of a project or to the people you are working with, then how can you expect others to be?

> Showing commitment to any of these is a demonstration of leadership.

Creativity
Leadership often requires creative thinking. Whether that is thinking laterally, thinking outside the box, recognizing options and opportunities or encouraging creative thinking in others.

> These aspects of creative thinking are demonstrations of leadership.

Communication
Effective leadership depends upon effective communication. Whether that is delivering instructions; succinctly getting ideas across; clearly stating the reality of a situation or encouraging and supporting the constructive

communication of other people.

> Being a good communicator in any of these areas is a demonstration of leadership.

Collaboration

This form of leadership means working collaboratively with people in the team, perhaps bringing people together in groups to work in mutual support of one another or seeking collaboration from people outside the community.

> A person able to inspire collaboration with and from others is demonstrating leadership.

Co-operation

Empowering leadership inspires cooperative working. The leader who does not work cooperatively with people in their team is likely to be more of a dictator than a leader. A leader who does not seek cooperation from those outside of the community may lead the community into a place of isolation and alienation from those whose support would be helpful or necessary.

> A person who is able to encourage and maintain co-operation within a community and/or is able to attract cooperation from others outside of the community is demonstrating leadership.

Consensus

Leadership does not mean taking all the decisions. Inspiring, supportive and empowering leadership results from ensuring that those who will carry out decisions have had a hand in making them, preferably, through consensus.

> A person encouraging and/or facilitating consensus decision making in a community is demonstrating leadership.

Courage

It often takes courage to be a leader. It can require courage to take on a role, to stand up and be counted or to say the things that need to be said when mindful of the potential consequences. It may need courage to take on responsibility. Especially if you are the only person to recognize there is some responsibility to take; if you might not be perceived as the obvious person to take it; or when others are unable or unwilling to do so.

The willingness to step forward in any of these circumstances is a demonstration of leadership.

Everyone is a potential leader

This is not just warm and fuzzy language! It is my belief based upon decades of experience.

> It seems obvious that in any situation the person with the appropriate skills, the appropriate information and/or experience; who has the appropriate attitude and intention and is willing to step forward at the appropriate time, is the obvious leader in that situation.

Whether or not the obvious person takes up a leadership role in any situation is usually dependent upon their courage, confidence and willingness to pick up the leadership baton at that time, and, whether the people they would be leading are willing to allow them to do so.

Being courageous

It may take courage for a person to offer himself or herself as a leader in a situation. Especially if they are new to a community or if there is a significant or obvious difference between them and the other members, such as age, gender, ethnic background, religion etc. A potential leader might be concerned that any action they would recommend might be unpopular with the rest of the community. If a person has seen others who have put themselves forward for leadership being metaphorically shot at, it may take great courage for them to risk putting themselves in the same position.

Being confident

For most of us, confidence in our abilities and in ourselves in general can take a long time to develop and yet can so quickly be undermined. I have seen talented people join communities with the very best of intentions, only to find their confidence in their abilities being eroded by the judgmental culture of the community and the critical and unsupportive attitudes of the members.

In some communities it may take a lot of self-confidence for some people to offer their skills, knowledge or experience, especially in those communities or groups which have a blame culture, where there is little mutual trust and loyalty or where the word 'leader' is assumed to mean boss.

If the community is unaware of the three stages of community development (described later) and/or the whole community or some members are stuck at the assertion stage, then the appropriate leaders for any situation are unlikely to be able to easily emerge.

Being willing

> The willingness to take the responsibility for leadership is what makes someone **into** a leader even if it's only for a short while or in particular circumstances.

Developing leadership strengths

Developing the leadership qualities of courage, confidence and willingness is essential personal development work. And, although it sometimes might be hard work, the rewards can be so great that every moment and every bit of effort is well worthwhile.

This work requires three things:
1. To know what you want to achieve.
2. The opportunities to practice.
3. The support and encouragement of at least one other person.

What do you want to achieve?

Perhaps they are some of the following:
a. Start a community or move a project forward.
b. Gain confidence and have the courage to offer ideas and suggestions.
c. Propose processes or actions.
d. Speak up in meetings.
e. Challenge existing ways of doing things or other people's ideas, perceptions or assumptions.

The opportunities to practice

Many of your everyday conversations can offer chances to practice communicating clearly and to try out strategies for getting ideas across, and for respectfully challenging statements or situations about which you have concerns. The group you are currently with could perhaps offer you plenty of opportunities to practice your courage and confidence in these areas.

However, if your previous experience with these people has been particularly uncomfortable or difficult, you might consider joining another group, maybe for a while, to flex your courage and confidence muscles in a new or more supportive setting.

Seeking support

You could seek the support and encouragement of a mentor or a coach. If neither of these is available to you, then find someone who would be willing to engage with you in mutual peer support. This could be someone in the same group or someone who has no involvement in it. You might find a person who is struggling with some of the same issues as yourself. You could perhaps find somebody who, although dealing with entirely different issues, would value some mutual support.

Doing the work

> The moves forward in developing yourself and your leadership skills need only be made in tiny steps. No giant leaps are needed or recommended.

Take a small step in one of the areas in which you wish to improve and see how it feels. Notice the response from others and then get some feedback from your support person. If something works well, do more of it. If something doesn't work well, do something different next time. If something you do feels too uncomfortable, explore with your support person why that might be. It could be just that the step you have taken was a bit too big at this point.

Practice makes perfect

In any area of development, the trick is to keep on keeping on. This is why the support of others is so valuable. It can prevent you from feeling alone and vulnerable and from doubting yourself, giving up or slipping into a decline if things don't go so well.

With practice, your levels of courage, confidence and willingness will grow. You will probably begin to wonder why you ever had any doubts in yourself or your leadership abilities. You may find yourself effortlessly assuming leadership roles, perhaps small at first, and then, with increased confidence, roles with greater responsibility and potential for making a difference. This may all be so seamless that people may not notice. If they do notice and remark upon it, by then you will have enough confidence to deal with whatever comes up.

Supportive leadership

> For a community, group or activity leader to be most effective, he or she, would be wise to use more elements of mentoring than managing, and place a greater emphasis on facilitation and upon coaching than upon controlling.

Some, possibly most, of the work with communities is often carried out by volunteers who are offering their time, skills and expertise in support of the community and for the benefit of the whole. The people in these working groups will thrive on encouragement and mutual respect. When people feel recognized for their abilities and trusted to use those abilities effectively they are more likely to continue to do so than when feeling doubted, distrusted overly managed or controlled.

Communities are likely to be less than effective when attitudes of criticism and disrespect lead to feelings of disempowerment among the group or community members. This also applies to negative attitudes, which can be harmful to the survival of a community. Negative attitudes could include: defeatism, aggression, undermining, sabotaging and the seeking of scapegoats.

> Attitudes that would be helpful in a community situation are: Cooperation, open-mindedness, honest and direct communication and compassion.

Timing

> An important part of being an effective leader is the comprehension of right timing.

Understanding the timing of strategies. Knowing when it is the right time to initiate a discussion or a process. Understanding the appropriate times to intervene or to hold back.

There are likely to be times when changes need to be made to the structure to fulfill the objectives of the project or even to guarantee its survival. Any inability on the part of the leader to recognize when the project has grown to the point where major changes are necessary could serious restrict the projects potential.

This understanding of timing includes knowing when it is time to release the reins of leadership into the hands of someone else.

Loyalty and leadership

Wise leaders know to place loyalty high on the group or community's agenda for achievement, and they set the example for loyalty within their community. They demonstrate loyalty at every opportunity: to the project, to the principles and agreements and most especially to every community member. Through this example, loyalty can become automatic among community members and an intrinsic part of the community culture.

Criticism of and jokes about the leader might be commonplace within groups of people who feel unhappy with a leader's decisions or disempowered by that person's style of leadership. Although this behavior might relieve feelings of frustration and even create some solidarity within the group, nonetheless, it is an example of disloyalty. It is even more so if those criticisms and jokes are taken outside of the group. How will this help? This type of behavior might do more damage to the group or community's effectiveness and success than the actions of the leader being criticized.

It seems to me that within many communities there is no place for the 'us' and 'them' attitudes of separation that exist in many hierarchical structures. This sense of separation easily allows for blame to be placed on the 'others'. People in communities thrive on the belief that, 'we are all in this together'. Everyone in a community can contribute towards this sense of togetherness.

It may take a lot of courage for some people in a group to bring their concerns and distress about the quality of leadership to the notice of the leader, especially an authoritarian leader, and yet, it might be difficult for the group to be effective or even to survive if this is not done.

You can make the difference through leadership

You could be an example of leadership that would offer encouragement to others to find or develop their leadership qualities. It can often just take one person to make a significant difference to a community by doing something different, to take the initiative, to speak up, to ask a question, to make a suggestion, to be positive and supportive.

> It often only takes one person to show the way for a community to consist of people who are willing to take responsibility for making things happen, who are able to step into appropriate leadership roles whenever necessary while having the support and confidence of the other members, and to encourage others to do the same.

It is clear that the abilities of leadership are not limited to only a few people in any community. The necessary skills of leadership can be learned and the attitudes and qualities can be encouraged and cultivated. This can help to alleviate concerns about the succession of any leadership role within any community situation and will support continuity.

7

DEVELOPING THE COMMUNITY CULTURE

It is apparent that all societies have a culture that immerges out of the strongest elements within it and which evolves over time. This also applies to all forms of community, whatever their nature.

Obviously, community cultures will differ from one another because they will be made up of different people with different attitudes, in different circumstances, in different places and with different purposes, objectives and resources. Even so, it is my experience that for the people in any community to have a sufficient degree of cooperation and harmonious interaction with one another, enough successful outcomes of actions and decisions, and some real potential for sustainability, the following elements will be essential:

> ➤ An understanding of the stages of development that any community will inevitably go through.
> ➤ Comprehension and agreement of intention, purpose and objectives. (This was covered earlier.)
> ➤ Agreement on some shared values ethics and how these will be reflected in the behavior, working practices, interactions, discussions and decisions.
> ➤ Respectful, effective and supportive interpersonal communications.
> ➤ Inclusive and productive meetings.

> ➤ Inclusive, cooperative and preferably consensus decision-making (also covered earlier).

Understanding community development

There are usually three main stages in the development of any community: The Inclusive Stage, the Assertive Stage, and finally the Co-operative Stage.

Each of these stages can have significant impact on any community or project and upon the individuals within them. The identification of each stage would be useful to support the effectiveness of most communities and initiatives and could be essential in supporting the sustainability of some.

With awareness, these stages can be easily identified. By paying attention to the behavior of members and the dynamics within the community it may become obvious which stage of development has been reached.

A closed community is a rare thing. Most communities are open to people joining and leaving the community at any time. All community projects and community-led regeneration initiatives will have people joining and leaving all the time. This means that whilst the community or initiative has a life of its own with identifiable stages of inclusion, assertion and cooperation, each individual joining at any of these stages of the development are likely to have an impact upon the process. They will go through the same stages in their integration into the group or community.

Stage 1. Inclusion

This is when people are finding their place as part of a group or community. Anxiety, shyness and introversion are common and the fear of rejection and the need for acceptance can be strong. People might not be fully productive in this phase as their focus may be on the desire to fit in and be accepted.

On the face of it, for most of us, the wish to feel included in any community to which we belong might seem to be just a matter of preference. However, the need to feel included may be stronger than we first imagine.

The need to fit in and to be accepted by the group and/or community to which we belong seems to be deeply ingrained in human beings. It probably has its origins in humanity's distant past when societies were arranged along recognized tribal lines. The tribe provided protection, food, care and support. Individuals living outside of the tribal community might have been vulnerable to many dangers and being excluded from the tribe could have been life threatening.

These days, apart from a few remaining pockets of tribal existence around the planet, being in or out of a community is rarely life-threatening, with the possible exception of extremist communities such as those involved in political violence, violent crime and gang warfare. Even so, it is a natural condition for we human beings to want to be accepted within our communities.

> The fear of being excluded or rejected can greatly influence behavior.

This need to belong can make people vulnerable to the behavior of others, especially to unkind behavior of other insecure people. This unkind behavior can include unwelcoming attitudes, bullying, gossiping and demeaning remarks.

> To avoid this, it would be wise for groups and communities to be formed with some conscious awareness of the need to foster attitudes of welcome and inclusion and of processes that help to build trust and good relationships.

Fitting in

Some people seem to have the ability to fit comfortably into any group. They feel at ease wherever they are and with any person they are with. Those who do not may have a variety of ways of attempting to fit in. They may be eager to seem friendly. They might show a willingness to do whatever is required of them. They can seem happy to conform to the values and ethics and the culture of the community or they may feel obliged to do so. They might appease people in leadership or dominant roles. They may slip into quiet acquiescence.

Some people spend much of their lives in this desire for inclusion and so devote a lot of time and energy to these 'being acceptable' types of attitudes and behavior. Those whose life experience has left them feeling excluded or always on the outside may need a lot of re-assurance before they feel fully accepted by others.

> For a few people there might not be sufficient assurance. These people might never leave the inclusion phase, no matter how long they are members of a group or community.

Individual self-management

You can make the difference to your group or community by developing an attitude of welcoming newcomers and by being aware of and managing any of your own exclusion types of behavior - such as ignoring newcomers or excluding them from conversations, being disdainful or patronizing and making remarks intended to hurt or embarrass.

If you are normally shy or reticent to speak with people you do not know well, you can use the opportunity of being in a community to make efforts to develop your social skills. You can be encouraged in this through the tolerance and understanding of other compassionate community members.

The leadership role in creating inclusion

The tone and the example that a leader sets in this inclusion stage is very important as this may quickly become the accepted norm for the group or community. The way in which all newcomers are welcomed will affect how well they are accepted, how quickly they become integrated and how effective their contribution to the community will be.

Introductions

When the community or initiative is forming or when newcomers are joining, it is important that the introduction of potential members is done with some conscious awareness.

> It would be helpful to have some process to assist people to connect easily with one another, which can then form the basis for the development of good working relationships.

There are useful introductory processes in our book: ENJOYABLE AND EFFECTIVE MEETINGS in the YOU MAKE THE DIFFERENCE series, which is available as paperback and e-book from Amazon, and is accessible through our website: www.youmakethedifference.net

If people are left to their own devices to connect with one another then cohesion is likely to take an unnecessary length of time. If newcomers are not carefully introduced into an existing group or community the cohesion can be disrupted. Unless there is a recognized inclusion process or the newcomer is experienced in groups, he or she might take time to become a useful member.

On the other hand, if newcomers are introduced with over enthusiastic reference to their talents and experience, some members of the existing group or community may feel that their place in it is under some kind of threat. Their behavior towards newcomers might be influenced by feelings of insecurity.

> People feeling insecure may attempt to mask that with attitudes of indifference, condescension or aggression.

This can make it difficult for new people to feel accepted and to easily offer their contribution.

Inclusive language

In most everyday communication it is usually beneficial to use 'I' statements. This gives the responsibility for the thoughts and feelings expressed in a statement to the person making it. This can help to prevent confrontation and any need for self-defense. However, in creating inclusion and maintaining cohesion in communities, it can be helpful to use a lot of inclusive language such as the words 'we' and 'us' and 'our' when referring to attitudes, behavior, decisions and actions within the community.

The pecking order

This inclusive stage is traditionally where the pecking order in a group or community starts to be recognized. The polite term for this is the 'establishment of roles and functions', however, the words are often nicer than the actions. In the inclusion stage people who consider themselves to be leaders will usually make that evident. However, in less confident people or those who are manipulative - often the same thing - this jostling for position is usually covert.

Eventually, most people reach the point where they feel included, accepted, at ease and comfortable within the group or community. This is when another stage emerges - that of individual assertion.

Stage 2. Assertion

It will be important to be aware that care needs to be taken at this time!

This can be the time for extending personal boundaries and of establishing greater degrees of personal power. It is a phase in which people reveal their strengths and might attempt to use what they consider to be other people's weaknesses to gain some advantage and where assertion can easily turn into aggression. These types of behavior may be tolerable in business organizations where people might feel obliged to climb over each other for advancement. I believe there is no place for them in intentional communities or community initiatives.

> There seems little point in working to improve the quality of life in communities if we lose the quality of ourselves along the way.

Time to assert

This is the time in a community's development when people feel confident enough within the community to share their wilder ideas, to put forward more radical suggestions, to be creative and to think outside the box. It is also the time when people feel ready and able to challenge the ideas and suggestions of others, especially leaders, and to question the way things are done.

This is the time when timid mice can occasionally turn into roaring lions. When people who have always gone along with the crowd become stubborn, argumentative, difficult, and suddenly seem to want their own way. When quiet acquiescence - that may have evolved into silent resentment - suddenly is no longer silent. When the people who have previously had little to say make very sensible suggestions and come up with brilliant ideas.

> These are rarely new characteristics that are emerging; they have usually been there all along. They have been held in check in the inclusion stage until people felt confident or safe enough to reveal them.

Double-edged

The assertion stage can be another double-edged sword! On one edge it can be a time of great creativity and energy as people get the bit between their teeth and move powerfully towards the community's objectives. This can be a competitive phase when a community may make up in productivity for what it loses in cohesion.

On the other edge, cracks may begin to appear within the fabric of the community. This can be a time of discord, when judgments and criticisms are thrown around; when decisions can be difficult to reach; when people might be accused of being awkward and when meetings can become lengthy, inconclusive and unpleasant.

This can be a time when people leave the group or community because they feel uncomfortable, frustrated or disappointed. This can result in a greater workload falling on fewer and increasingly over-stretched individuals. This can be when progress just limps along or grinds to a halt. This can be a stage where communities and initiatives fail.

Not the end

In the communities where there is little or no understanding of the three stages of community development it may seem at this stage that the community is falling apart at the seams. It may feel as though the harmony and the co-operation within the community have disappeared and have been replaced by aggression and dysfunction. This is rarely the case. The harmony and cooperation that seem to have disappeared might not have been there in any real depth in the first place. There may have been only an artificial, pretend, on-the-surface, kind of harmony and co-operation that vanished when people felt themselves to be an integral part of the community and became confident enough to allow their real characteristics to show up.

This is not the end. In terms of building cohesion, this is the stage when the real work begins!

Permanent state of assertion

There are people who spend most of their time in assertive types of behavior. They seem rarely to have the need to feel included and accepted. They want and often expect to get their own way in all things and are likely to be persistent until they do. They may never become really cooperative; believing as they do that cooperation is something that others ought to offer to them.

Even though assertion might be essential if things are going to get done, permanently assertive people can cause havoc in communities. Words that are sometimes used to describe permanently assertive people are: bullies, power hungry, control freaks, dictators, demanding, awkward and insensitive. These people are often considered to be difficult to have in any group or community.

Concerns about having to deal with 'difficult' people are frequently cited as the reason why some people leave groups or communities or do not join them in the first place.

Mo

In Findhorn I had a dear friend, Mo, who through a permanent state of assertiveness achieved a great deal in her life, although it also caused difficulties in her relationships and diminished her popularity in the eyes of some people in our community. With the help of her friends, she became less difficult to be with, without losing any of her effectiveness. As she gradually became more able to see herself as others saw her, she modified her behavior to some extent, which made it easier for more people to support her projects. She put a notice where she and others could see it that stated, 'I am not obnoxious; I am just tact challenged!'

The leadership role in managing assertiveness

> When over-assertive people are the leaders of group or communities, other members may be treated more as followers than peers.

Although extremely assertive leaders can get things done, they often leave the wreckage of bruised egos in their wake. They might achieve objectives only by railroading through ideas and by riding roughshod over other people's ideas and suggestions, protests and objections.

Through honest communication regarding concerns about such a person's attitudes, community members can help these people to manage these tendencies and become more respectful in their behavior.

It could be beneficial to use some of the methods described in the chapter on handling tricky situations in the book, ENJOYABLE & EFFECTIVE MEETINGS in this series. This is available in paperback and e-book formats from Amazon and is accessible through our website: www.youmakethedifference.net

This important and valuable development phase can be tough on a leader. There may often be disagreements within the group or community and challenges to their leadership. Unfortunately, some leaders feel threatened by challenges, and so feel distressed or develop the need to assert their authority and to keep in control.

I believe it is wise for a leader to allow some challenges to be made and upheld. An effective leader can encourage people to satisfy their assertion needs appropriately, to take responsibilities for their behavior and to balance their own needs with those of the community. Effective leadership is a balancing act in these circumstances. If a leader displays openness and honesty and discloses some of his or her concerns and feelings or even some vulnerability, others may follow suit and good relating practices based upon integrity, self-disclosure and authenticity could be established.

> Effective leaders will juggle the needs of individuals to assert themselves; the needs of the community as a whole; the ultimate community objectives; and their own needs as leader as they support the community towards the cooperative stage.

Assertion may well be necessary to get things done, however, unless assertion is managed well the community may never move beyond this stage, which could have unfortunate results. For the cooperative stage to be reached, the dominating and controlling aspects of assertion need to be minimized or well managed.

Individual self-management

> Extreme assertion can quickly become aggression; and assertion over people who are in some way vulnerable is bullying.

Being assertive does not mean belittling or demeaning people, nor does it mean being argumentative and it certainly does not mean being rude, verbally abusive or deliberately obstructive.

You can make the difference in your community by demonstrating how to avoid falling into these traps and assisting others to pay attention to the way that they assert themselves in any community situation.

Questions about ideas, queries about the methods of doing things or the offering of suggestions and differing opinions can be done respectfully and constructively. Constructive communication, direct speech, creative suggestions, positive thinking and inspiring presentations are appropriate and powerful ways of being assertive in a community.

Self-assertion about ideas and suggestions may take courage for some people at first.

Community situations where everyone is working towards a common goal can be a very supportive environment in which to try out and develop some assertiveness.

More confident members of the community could offer understanding, tolerance and compassion towards those who are attempting and perhaps struggling to improve these skills.

It would be wise to keep in mind that co-operation can be built upon a balance of the positive aspects of inclusion and well-managed assertion.

Stage 3. Cooperation

> When the community feels inclusive enough for most members to express themselves with appropriate assertion then co-operation can quickly follow.

Individual self-management in co-operation

Co-operation in groups or communities requires the following elements:

1. Mutual trust and regard between those involved.
2. Recognition of and a respect for the skills and characteristics of all those involved.
3. A commitment from all those involved to be supportive to one another.
4. Clear, honest and respectful communication between those involved.
5. Willingness to compromise in order to reach the community's objectives.

The achievement of the groups or community's objectives is more likely once co-operation is established because decisions can be reached with greater speed and ease; communications are likely to be more honest and straightforward; those involved will understand their roles and carry them out with conviction, and each person takes full responsibility for their behavior and their actions.

The leadership role in co-operation

Harmony might exist for much of the time once co-operation is reached, although, the most productive communities can be highly co-operative and yet may retain a degree of dynamic tension. The most effective leaders preserve this with sensitivity. Apart from this, there is likely to be very little the leader may need to do to manage the community or initiative at this stage. The role can become more one of facilitation than management. This could include such things as:

> ➤ Having an overview of the community's activities in relationship to the objectives.
> ➤ Encouraging members of the community to take a leadership role in their area of interest or activity.
> ➤ Providing opportunities for discussions and the sharing of information.
> ➤ Facilitating some or all of the meetings.

Facilitation includes engaging in processes to improve communication and to support community decision-making. Some of the information in the book EFFORTLESS FACILITATION in this series could be helpful. This is available in paperback and as an e-book from Amazon and is accessible through our website: www.youmakethedifference.net

Individual contributions to community development

Obviously, individuals respond differently from one another in the various stages of their community's development. Some people have a real need to feel included before they are able to feel comfortable in a group or community situation. Some are rarely anything other than assertive. Yet others quickly reach and easily maintain a cooperative attitude. Most people will go through each stage to some degree in their community activities. It will be useful for people to be aware of these stages within themselves and when other members are demonstrating them.

> Recognizing people's behavior is not to make them out to be wrong in any way. It is to realize that we are all human, that we each have our own ways of dealing with situations and making life work for us.

Communities are like families and intimate relationships in that they provide many opportunities for self-awareness and personal development through the interactions between those involved. No matter how committed any of us are to a community or a project; no matter how strong our intentions might be to keep our less admirable behavior and characteristics from detrimentally affecting other people; at some stage, all of ourselves will show up. How well this is dealt with individually and collectively can determine how well a community will succeed.

It is obviously possible for communities to fulfill their purpose without anyone in them being aware of these three stages of community development. However, many communities without this information struggle along, often in strife or frustration and without much joy in their activities and interactions.

For a group or a community to survive for any length of time, to effectively achieve its purpose and to provide an enjoyable and rewarding experience for its members, it is beneficial for at least one of those involved to have this knowledge and be strong enough to use it. This might be, although does not need to be, the overall leader of the community.

> You can make the difference to your community by developing your self-awareness and to make conscious choices regarding your attitudes and behavior in each of these stages, and, by helping your community colleagues to do the same.

Those people in community initiatives who reach the stage of working together co-operatively usually really enjoy the experience and get a great deal out of it. So much so that, even when the original purpose for their coming together has been achieved, they may choose to find other reasons for continuing to meet and to work together as a group.

People starting up or living in intentional communities and those developing local community initiatives have the opportunity to consciously create the kind of culture that will be most supportive to their members and citizens; a culture that will help them and their community to flourish and be sustainable.

Agreement on values ethics and behavior

When a community or a group is clear about its values and ethics it is likely to attract to it the people who have those same values and ethics.

When an individual is looking for a community or an organization to work with they will usually be looking for one that has the same values and ethics that they hold dear. This also often applies to funders and other supporters.

I find it surprising how few of us go about our work and daily lives without consciously developing a set of personal values and ethics that influences our decisions and underpins our actions and behavior. Many of us have a spiritual or religious belief that includes strong values and ethics, and yet, are these always held consciously? How often are these demonstrated in all of our thoughts, words and deeds?

When there is a lack of consciousness about personal values and ethics, it is perhaps not so surprising that many communities and organizations do not engage in processes to identify what underpins their work. In my experience, the identification and establishment of Values and Ethics of a community or a project is an essential element to support commitment, effective working practices, and, ultimately, sustainability. A process to establish these would be best done in frank and open discussion amongst all of the people involved.

> It is important that this process is not avoided or rushed. These values and ethics will underpin the actions of those involved and support appropriate decision-making.

When the values and ethics have been identified they can form the basis for the group or the community's agreements on practices and behavior. It is vital for an intentional community to be clear about what values and ethics will underpin their working and living together. Going through this process can be a useful way to discover the common ground or the differences between community members in regard to their values and ethics.

People will have different priorities or personal agendas, which will influence or be influenced by their personal values and ethics.

It is worth remembering that when people have been drawn together in the common cause of creating or sustaining a community, there is most likely to be enough similar threads of values and ethics among them that can be woven into an agreement to build the foundations of their community life and to hold them together.

If, at the start of a community coming together, processes are gone through to identify the community's values and ethics, this will go a long way towards bringing inclusion and cohesion to the community. This activity might be the most important work to establish the community and support its sustainability.

Having said that, it is never too late for an established community to identify and make agreements about their shared values and ethics. Some of the processes useful for this can be found in the books, ENJOYABLE & EFFECTIVE MEETINGS and in EFFORTLESS FACILITATION in this series.

> Although there will be specific values and ethics required for each community or initiative to effectively achieve its aims, there are a number that would be beneficial in any community: mutual respect, honesty, clarity, straightforwardness, tolerance, cooperation, taking responsibility, and willingness.

When these underpin the attitudes, the communication, behavior and actions of individuals and the community as a whole, that community is unlikely to go far wrong.

Making Agreements

When the values and ethics underpinning behavior and work within the community or initiative are identified and agreed upon, it will be wise and beneficial to put them into some form of statement for those involved to sign or to which they can make a verbal agreement or pledge.

Whether called Community Agreements, Intention, Commitment, Statement of Common Ground or anything else, this can be a great aid to maintaining cohesion, congruency and trust within the community. Knowing that colleagues, friends and neighbors have made the same agreements as one another improves people's attitudes towards openness and greater risk taking in self-expression.

The following example of a community agreement has been adapted from the Statement of Common Ground, first devised many years ago in the Findhorn Community and which is continuously being reviewed to reflect the evolution of that community. This has proved to be a useful template for the agreements made by many communities around the world.

Community Agreement

1. Support

I wholeheartedly support the aims of this community and the wellbeing and ongoing development of all community members - including myself.

2. Personal integrity and respect

I will maintain high standards of personal integrity, embodying congruence of thought, word and action. I will respect other people, their views, origins, backgrounds, issues and experiences.

3. Direct communication

I will use clear and honest communication with straightforwardness, attentive listening and respectful responses. In public and in private I will avoid speaking in any way that maligns or demeans others. I will talk to people rather than about them and will not seek to gossip or collude. I will challenge any actions, manipulation or intimidation that I feel may be detrimental to myself or to others.

4. Responsibility

I will take full responsibility for my thoughts, words and actions. I am willing to listen to constructive criticism and to offer constructive feedback to others in a caring and appropriate fashion that will support each of us to grow. I acknowledge that there may be wider perspectives than my own and deeper concerns than those that immediately affect me. I will take responsibility to work through or put aside my personal issues for the benefit of the whole community.

5. Conflict resolution

I will make every effort to resolve all personal and community conflict as soon as possible. In the event of a dispute continuing unresolved I will adhere to the community grievance procedure or I may call for an advocate, friend, independent observer, mediator or facilitator to support a mediated process.

6. Cooperation

I will work cooperatively within the community and consider other people's views carefully and respectfully. I recognize that others may make decisions that affect me and I agree to respect the care, integrity and wisdom that they have put into the decision-making process.

7. Commitment

I commit to keeping these agreements and to exercising the spirit of this statement in all my dealings.

Signature.

Date.

Obviously for those people engaged in a community project or community-led regeneration, the word 'community' in the statement could be replaced with the words 'group' or 'association', for example.

Challenging broken agreements

When a group or community has created a statement of values and ethics and behavior that each member has agreed or committed to, then anyone in the community will be in a position to challenge any other member whose behavior demonstrates a disregard for those values and ethics.

> The challenging of a person regarding their agreement can be more effective than directly challenging their behavior and certainly more supportive than making criticism or judgments.

Q

'How does this help?' is a useful question to ask a person whose actions are outside of their agreed parameters of the community's values, ethics, attitudes and behavior.

Influencing community culture

Leadership in the community culture

The culture of any community or initiative is likely to be heavily influenced by the leader or the founder, at least in the early stages of a community's existence. The attitudes and behavior that become part of the accepted culture will probably be set by the leader and then permeate through the rest of the community.

The leader who wants to dominate; who treats people with disrespect; is overly demanding and looks for people to blame when things go wrong, is likely to influence a culture of uncertainty and mistrust. In this type of culture, members of the community often behave critically and judgmentally towards each other; are cautious about offering suggestions and are likely to put most of their energy into self-protection and self-preservation.

On the other hand, if the leader is respectful, inclusive and communicative; is open to suggestions and shares decision-making, then the community culture will probably be one of mutual respect, which fosters a high degree of willingness to participate among those involved. Even so, this top-down influence of community culture can be changed or moderated by the influence of other members.

Everyone will have an influence on the culture

Community cultures are living things that are forever changing and adapting. All those involved can be leaders in influencing the development of the culture of the community:

- ➢ A person who knows about interpersonal communications can lead the community towards a culture of good communication.
- ➢ Someone having an understanding of community dynamics and community development can contribute this understanding to the community.
- ➢ A person with skills in efficiency or cooperative decision-making can offer these to the community.
- ➢ Someone who knows how to motivate, encourage and appreciate people can have a significant influence on creating a can-do culture.
- ➢ People whose attitudes encourage mutual high regard and trust can influence others to develop these attitudes.
- ➢ A person who is naturally kind and supportive towards others can, by demonstration, encourage these attitudes to become part of a community's culture.

If you have any of these skills and experience then you can make the difference in your community by positively influencing its culture. Reading this book is likely to help you to do this effectively.

Loyalty in Community

Loyalty is a powerful element in the culture of any community. When achieved, loyalty bonds a community together and creates a sense of common purpose that is extremely powerful and effective. To develop loyalty the people within a community need to identify closely with the vision, purpose, values and ethics of the community and most importantly with each other. The closer they identify the deeper the relationships can be; the stronger will be the harmony and bonding between them and the more successful and sustainable the community or project is likely to be.

Loyalty to each other is the most powerful antidote to 'blame cultures'. People are usually more willing to take responsibility and be accountable for their actions when they realize that making mistakes is a part of life that is best seen as learning opportunities. Learning from mistakes is far more likely to happen in a supportive environment when people help each other out when they most need it.

Taking the lead in loyalty

It does not have to be the overall leader who takes responsibility for creating a culture of loyalty in a community. Anyone within a community can take the lead in this.

> You can make the difference to your community by taking care how you communicate to and about others in the community. This will go a long way towards creating a loyalty culture.

This can be done through:
  a. Using respectful language in conversations and in discussions.
  b. Listen attentively and show that you value other people's opinions.
  c. Avoiding gossiping about other community members and discourage it in your colleagues.
  d. Speaking directly to people who have done or said things that have upset you rather than talking about them to others.
  e. Avoiding judging people.
  f. If some criticism feels necessary make it constructive criticism.

For some people, loyalty to others might be a new concept. In their places of employment, the communities and initiatives in which they have previously been engaged or even within their families, people might have experienced a strong blame culture. Self-preservation and protection against this is likely to have resulted in a diminished sense of loyalty. Some people might have experienced loyalty as being something demanded of them and yet rarely given to them.

Remember: Although the work of building loyalty in some community cultures might take time, the benefits to the community, to the individual members and to the success of the project, could be considerable.

Communication

The way in which people in a community or local initiative communicate with one another will say a lot about the culture of the community. When individuals join or are considering joining a group or community it might be wise for them to pay close attention to this. In my experience, the quality of communication within communities, organizations and projects has a significant effect upon the level of success. Because of this, the next chapter is devoted to it.

Meetings

Much of the work and many of the activities in communities take place in meetings. The quality of those meetings can determine how successful a community or any project within it will be.

Participant's attitudes towards community meetings can vary from positive enthusiasm to dread and avoidance, with most people somewhere in between. These attitudes usually result from experiences of meetings and of the quality and effectiveness of those events. If people have found the meetings they have attended to be dry, uninteresting, frustrating or disempowering they are not likely to want to participate again.

As engagement in community initiatives, projects, and activities increases, people who may never have previously attended meetings, might now choose to do so. Those who have had little or no experience of effective meeting participation could find useful suggestions for this in our GUIDE TO EFFECTIVE AND ENJOYABLE MEETINGS, which is available to download for free from our website: www.youmakethedifference.net.

Meeting Management

> For people to remain involved and engaged and to believe that they can make a meaningful contribution to their community, these meetings will need to be inclusive, effective, productive and enjoyable.

One of the difficulties is that relatively few people have excellent experiences of meetings or have good meeting management skills to bring to bear when called upon to manage meetings within their communities.

These skills are rarely part of a school curriculum, even though meetings are likely to play a significant part in most adults' lives. More surprisingly, little training in meeting management seems to be offered in most occupations. There appears to be an expectation that when a person is good at their job and is promoted to manager, team leader or some role which requires them to manage meetings, then the skills to do so effectively and effortlessly will suddenly emerge. So it is not surprising that these skills are not yet commonplace in community situations.

> For communities and initiatives to be sustainable, the meetings through which they are organized need to be well managed.

The skills to do so can be easily learned and implemented and can make the roles of chairperson or facilitator rewarding and fulfilling, especially when the outcomes improve situations or enhance lives.

It is for these reasons that the first two books to be published in the YOU MAKE THE DIFFERENCE series were on meetings.

Information of all aspects of meetings can be found in ENJOYABLE & EFFECTIVE MEETINGS. This book offers guidelines for participation in and for the management of several types of meetings. It includes information on essential procedures, methods for decision-making, on many useful processes and how to use them in tricky situations.

Included in the second book, EFFORTLESS FACILITATION, are suggestions for designing and planning facilitated meetings and events, information on methods, procedures and processes, and insights into making facilitation effortless. There are also some ready-made meeting designs that could be adapted for many community situations. Both of these books are in paperback and e-book versions and available from Amazon and through our website: www.youmakethedifference.net

Effective meetings

Obviously the purpose of any meeting is to bring two or more people together to achieve defined outcomes. These outcomes may be wide ranging, such as developing ideas for community regeneration, or be very specific e.g. allocating budgets to projects.

> A fully effective meeting will achieve its purpose to the satisfaction of its participants in a smooth and efficient manner. It will complete the agenda, make sensible decisions and have beneficial outcomes. An enjoyable meeting will be interesting; everyone attending will feel included and valuable and have an equal opportunity to be heard and to contribute.

Whatever the form the meeting takes there will be a requirement for some element of planning and management. The quality of the management of any meeting can have a huge influence on the outcomes. Poorly managed meetings can result in the ineffectiveness of a group or organization, the frustration and dissatisfaction of the participants and potentially the failure of a project. Well-managed meetings usually result in outcomes leading to the success of projects, the on-going effectiveness of community groups, and leave participants feeling satisfied that they have spent their time wisely and productive.

Whether a meeting is for a few colleagues to briefly check in with one another on the progress of their work or a large gathering of people considering the future of their town, a high quality of the meeting management is vital.

> You could make an enormous difference to your community by helping to develop a supportive and efficient meeting culture.

The quality of the community experience

The feel good factor

For most people, feeling good in their community means feeling included and believing that they are a recognized member of the community; that they have some influence on what happens in the community; believing that they will be heard in meetings, that their views will be taken seriously and knowing that they will participate in at least some of the decision-making.

In my experience, a vitally important element of the feel good factor is feeling fulfilled by the community experience.

Fulfillment

There are many ways in which people can feel fulfilled through their community activities. Although each individual will have specific aspects to their sense of fulfillment there are some elements that are likely to be common to most:

    a.   The sense of achieving a purpose.
    b.   Feeling a part of something important.
    c.   Being involved in a successful project or effective group.
    d.   Pride in providing much needed help or support.
    e.   Belief that all their efforts have been worthwhile.
    f.   The recognition that their involvement has made a difference.

Being valued and appreciated

> Feeling valued in a community for most people means knowing that their contribution is respected and that their time, efforts and abilities are recognized.

It could be useful to remember that the less control people have over the decisions that affect their work and activities, the more appreciation they are likely to need in order to remain committed and enthusiastically involved. Unfortunately, there is a commonly held belief that service is its own reward and that people ought not to seek recognition or appreciation for offering their time, effort and skills to a community or an initiative they believe in.

> In my experience, any community or initiative that operates under this illusion is likely to have some less than enthusiastic members and volunteers who may not stay around for very long.

Those who do stay may be doing so out of loyalty to friends or colleagues or a deep commitment to the cause. Any advantage taken of such people will ultimately tarnish even the most laudable of causes.

By choice

People in the business and public sectors are often obliged to work together and to get on with one another as best they can. These people may be able to do so because this is what is expected of them by their employers or by the public. And/or they benefit financially, directly or indirectly, from the work of their colleagues; and/or through mutual respect for the skills, professionalism and experience of one another.

It is important to remember that in many intentional communities and most local initiatives people are giving their time freely to carry out many of the activities. They are offering their skills, expertise and experience because they want to make a contribution.

Everyone involved can show appreciation to one another in many ways.

> Simple, direct, authentic, immediate and specific appreciation of those around you will work wonders on so many levels.

Small appreciations

A nod of acknowledgment or a word of thanks for things done well, completed on time or with good humor can let people know that their daily efforts are noticed and appreciated. This is not just something for leaders to do. Everyone in a community could contribute to an appreciative culture by behaving this way with one another. However, leaders can make a significant contribution by taking time in meetings and discussions to acknowledge and appreciate effective and efficient work.

Specific Appreciations

Appreciation and praise ought to be expressed as specifically as possible. Telling someone they are 'great' does not really tell them much about what is so great about them or what they are doing; and is often a hollow or meaningless form of praise. The point to appreciation is to let people know what has been noticed and valued about them and their work. Using expressions such as: 'Thank you for...' 'I appreciate the way you...' 'I can see how much you have...' 'This will help me to...' 'I am grateful to you for finishing this so quickly: it gives me plenty of time to put this information into the report', will make this clear. Knowing what it is that they do well helps people to feel good and do more of it.

Immediate Appreciation

> Praise and appreciation ought to be given as soon as possible after the event.

A delay that separates the appreciation from the action might make it less meaningful. Saving the praising of someone until a community meeting is likely to have a less beneficial effect on that person if in the meantime he or she has been feeling unappreciated. Do both! Tell the person immediately and then express the same appreciation in the later meeting.

Authentic Appreciation

I have noticed a tendency towards the use of over exaggeration in praise and appreciation such as Wow! Fantastic! Fabulous! Etc. Far from expressing a depth of appreciation, these words have lost much of their power from over use.

The same goes for the use of jargon. The fashion in the use of descriptive words probably changes more rapidly within cultures than in any other aspect of communication. Most age communities and common interest communities invent their own language of appreciation. Gear! Cool! Awesome! Wicked! These are examples of words that have been in and out of fashion in recent times. Using this kind of jargon is meaningless to anyone outside any specific culture. Doing so when the words are out of fashion, are not valued by the person you are praising or are not your usual way of speaking may make you appear ingenuous.

Direct Appreciation

> Praise a person to their face.

Telling other people how much you appreciate someone and hoping that information will reach that person will at best dilute that appreciation and make it less effective and at worst not reach the intended recipient at all. Do both! Tell the person and then tell others as well.

When appreciation is at the core of a community's culture then the people in that community are likely to be supportive of one another and be willing to go the extra mile.

Creativity

Creativity in the Arts

The visual arts, dance, music and drama offer opportunities for expression and bring people together in mutual enjoyment and appreciation. Communities can provide a safe and supportive environment for artists and performers of all disciplines to experiment, to take chances, and to expand the boundaries of their talents and experience. Through some of these mediums individuals and a community as a whole can explore themes that matter to them, sometimes in a more acceptable or a less confrontational way than through dialogue.

> Being creative in the visual aspects of a community is important.

I have observed communities struggling for existence in hardly adequate dwellings or in drab surroundings where spirits have been lifted and perseverance encouraged by the creativity of some of the people involved. Even small expressions of creativity can raise the ordinary or mundane to heights of visual pleasure and inspiration.

The built environment

This is obviously a place for creativity. Ecovillages, and most forms of intentional community these days, intend to be ecological and are committed to environmental sustainability. Eco-friendly building materials are usually still more expensive and sometimes more difficult to obtain than traditional materials. As these types of communities are often financially challenged it requires some creative thinking for them to achieve their construction goals while keeping to their environmental commitments. This also applies to their intention to re-cycle, repair and re-use goods and materials.

Some communities devote a great deal of time, effort and resources into constructing some major building that makes a big statement about who they are. An example of this is the Matramandia, the meditation hall in Auroville in South East India. This hall is an enormous, glorious sphere with an interior of white marble and an exterior of large disks covered in gold leaf.

Other communities concentrate their design and architectural creativity on building or improving the homes of their members. This might be as varied as new construction developments such as a CoHousing project or an Ecovillage or through improving caravans and trailers to be more eco-friendly or to become habitable all year round.

In some communities inspiring creativity has been used to make homes out of derelict buildings or from local, cheap, found or free materials such as straw bales, adobe bricks, fallen trees and drift-wood, earth-filled tires and glass bottles.

Creating with color

It is amazing the difference that can be made by the introduction of color in communities living and working in uninspiring surroundings. This is often achieved through planting flowers in gardens or in containers and having plants climbing walls or hanging from baskets wherever possible. Much improvement can also be made through the use of colored paint on parts of, or the whole of, some or all the buildings. This can have such a visual impact that it might be wise to seek advice from a color expert.

> The appearance of uninspiring or unlikely looking buildings can be beautifully and economically improved through some lovely effects created from paints of a small pallet of complimentary colors.

Individuality

Occasionally I come across the belief that to create an egalitarian community it is necessary for all the dwellings in it to be of the same design, with only small variations in size, and where there are rules limiting the personalizing of them by their occupants. While I understand the economy of scale in this approach to building, I have concerns about the wisdom of limiting people's personal expression regarding their own homes.

I realize that having identical dwellings as the social leveling factor in community may sometimes be intended to create a sense of equality among people from different social and economic backgrounds. However I wonder if there is a danger that this strategy might prevent some people who have a strong sense of individualism and personal style and/or have been financially successful from joining such a community or participating in such a project. I believe this could be a pity, and be detrimental in the long term, because it is my experience that people with these attributes can make all sorts of significant contributions to a community's sustainability.

It seems to me that it is in the communing – the coming together of hearts and minds of people - where community and equality are created. This is where and how social and economic differences become immaterial. When discussion, common agreements, shared activities, everyday interactions and specific processes lead to mutual understanding and respect then old paradigm attitudes and traditional ways of judging the status or measuring the value of people can change. When that happens within a strong sense of community, it can help people to move beyond any feelings of inadequacy about what they don't have or any feelings of envy, resentment or criticism towards people who have more. It might also support some individuals to grow beyond feeling the need, or obliging others, to diminish themselves in any way in order to fit in.

Creative thinking

> Many aspects of community life will benefit from creative thinking.

Thinking outside the box, seeking a variety of options, looking for alternative solutions and approaches to situations and exploring radical ideas can make community life exciting. It is my experience that community engagement offers opportunities for creative thinking that may be rarely available to many people. Thinking creatively together about the things that really matter to them can be very empowering for individuals and be supportive of a community culture of collaboration.

Celebration

Celebration has always been an important aspect of community life. Probably as far back as when we were living in caves we humans have enjoyed coming together for celebration. In any group of people there will be many things to celebrate: achievements, successes, birthdays, anniversaries and rites of passage. Throughout the year there will be opportunities for seasonal and religious festivals and to mark days of significance.

> The richer the national and ethnic mix in a community, the greater the opportunities for celebration there are likely to be as people contribute festivals and celebrations from their traditional culture to that of the culture they are creating together.

When life is a struggle or when there is so much work to do to keep a community project on track it might sometimes feel that there is very little to celebrate or very little time, or money, to do so. These are exactly the times when celebrations are most needed and beneficial! While some effort might be made around such things as religious festivals, many celebrations do not need to be elaborate affairs. A cake and a song to celebrate a birthday or a few moments to celebrate the completion of some stage of a building project can bring pleasure to individuals, lift spirits and encourage people to keep on keeping on.

It could be beneficial to have an individual or a group of people responsible for initiating or coordinating celebrations in the community. Having creative people in such a group can turn even the simplest of celebrations into occasions of delight.

It is worth remembering that communities who have a culture of celebration are ones that usually have a high level of cooperation and cohesion and are likely to be attractive for people to engage in.

Creativity and celebration are such important aspects in community culture. In the book: FINDHORN COMMUNITY FABLES - a collection of over 100 stories about the Findhorn Community - so many of the stories submitted by people were about creativity and celebration that I devoted two chapters to these topics. This is available from Amazon and through our website: www.youmakethedifference.net

Commitment

Some people have no difficulty in making commitment. Whether this is to something or someone they care about; to the decisions they have made, to stepping up to their responsibilities or to keeping their word. On the other hand, some people obviously have a great deal of difficulty in making and keeping to any form of commitment. Most people's attitude towards commitment seems to be somewhere in the middle.

During several decades working as a life coach I have listened to many clients who have had difficulty making or keeping commitments. For some this was about the worthiness of the project or the person they were reluctant to commit to and for others it seemed to be more about their own feelings of self-worth.

Many people seemed to feel genuine fear of commitment. Some people had the fear that making a commitment would limit their freedom and that it would somehow restrict their rights or their individuality. For others, the fear was more in their doubts about themselves. Doubts that they would be able to keep their commitments and/or doubts about their ability to live up to expectations—theirs or other people's.

Of course, some people did not really believe in what they were being required to make a commitment to, or really wanted the relationship, the job or the lifestyle in question.

The level of people's commitment to a community or an initiative is likely to determine how successful it will be.

It will also make a difference to how supportive they are to the project and the people within it, how well they can be relied upon and the amount of trust people will place in them. What people often don't realize is that the amount of pleasure and fulfillment they get out of their involvement is usually equal to the level of commitment they make.

I am of the opinion that my life belongs to the whole community and as long as I live, it is my privilege to do for it whatever I can.
George Bernard Shaw

Commitment to the purpose and objectives

When individuals fully comprehend and make their commitment to the intention, purpose and objectives of the community or the initiative this provides a firm foundation upon which to make decisions and take action.

Commitment to agreements

When everyone involved has made their commitment to the agreed common ground of values, ethics and behavior this supports the development of mutual trust.

Commitment to one another

In making their commitment to one another the people involved in any form of community demonstrate their willingness to be relied upon.

We do not so much need the help of our friends as the confidence of their help in need.
Epicurus

Commitment to excellence

> When people choose to be involved in a community they are likely to have a strong commitment to achieving excellence in all aspects of it.

I believe that all communities deserve the same commitment to the levels of excellence from those involved as might be found in organizations that provide products and services for which they are well paid. In this commitment to excellence in community it ought to make no difference whether the people working in these communities are paid or volunteers.

Commitment to continuity

In making their commitment to continuity people show that they are willing to step up to take responsibility when required and to support fellow community members to do the same.

Courage

It can take courage to be involved in and to make a commitment to any form of community.

It can take courage to step up and take responsibility; to think outside the box; to do things differently; to try new ways of managing, of making decisions and of taking action. It can take courage to think beyond our own needs in being supportive to others within the bigger picture. It can take courage to have the desire and the intention to make a difference in our communities. It can take extreme courage when to do so might be risky or dangerous.

Conscious awareness

The level of our willingness and eagerness to become engaged in our community indicates the level of our conscious awareness of the bigger picture. The levels of our understanding of who we each are; of how we behave, of how we relate to other individuals, to our community and to the world is an indication of the level of our maturity as people. In being consciously aware of all of these, and of what improvements could be made within ourselves and within society supports our wisdom in making decisions and taking action towards sustainability.

Beware of separation and elitism

In developing the culture of a community care ought to be taken to avoid the traps of separation and elitism.

I have noticed that when people have worked hard and consciously to develop a high quality culture within their community there is sometimes a tendency towards elitist thinking. This can happen when those in a community feel that the culture of that community or their initiative somehow makes them different from or better than other people, and separates them from those outside of the community or who are not involved in the initiative.

There may be a reluctance to let some people into an intentional community or to be involved in an initiative because there is a belief that 'they won't fit in' or 'they will not know how to do things our way.' There may even be a feeling, perhaps not directly expressed, that some people are 'not good enough' in some way to be a member of a community. There might be some criticism of newcomers for doing things or for behaving in ways that the established community has moved beyond, 'That's not how we do things.'

It seems to me that using this 'they are not like us' approach as a way of maintaining separateness from others is not an example of conscious development; it is more an example of entrenched and outdated human behavior. It is these 'we are better than them' and 'they are less than us' attitudes that have separated people by race and religion, by color and creed, for millennia. I believe that there is no place for this type of thinking in any society.

> Establishing a community culture that has high values and ethics does not mean that the people in that community are better than others. I suspect that if some sort of sense of superiority exists in a community's culture then there is still some work to be done on that community's values and ethics.

This applies especially to intentional communities where the culture might be different to that of the culture of the area or the country around them. If an intentional community's culture is significantly different in such things as religion, politics, education, and in attitudes and beliefs towards the environment, money, education, sex, ownership and the like, to those of other locals, there is likely to be a distinct sense of separation between that community and the people in the surrounding area. This could pose problems for both groups.

If the culture of an intentional community is considered to be alien by the folk in the local area this may result in suspicion and their reluctance to engage. If this difference is compounded by a belief in their own superiority by people in an intentional community, this may result in them being resented and alienated, or at least very unpopular with their neighbors. If these differences of culture are left unattended the resulting feelings of separation between such groups of people can remain for years, even decades.

People who are attracted to a community or an initiative that has consciously developed a culture of high values etc. are usually willing to work within that community's agreements and guidelines. They may already have the same values and ethics as those in that community or are ready to embrace them. Perhaps their values and ethics might be even higher than those of the community. Some people might benefit from compassionate support as they learn and adopt the community's guidelines for communication and behavior. This attitude of compassionate support towards all members would most likely be built-in to a community that has consciously created a supportive culture.

It would be wise to remember that culture which helps a community to effectively and enjoyably achieve its aims while supporting the ongoing development of its members is a culture that could be an inspirational model in any society.

By becoming consciously aware of all the aspects covered in this chapter and the following one, you can make a significant difference to your community. By embodying and demonstrating these aspects you can inspire others to have the courage to make the commitment do the same.

8

CONSTRUCTIVE COMMUNICATION

> The quality of the day-to-day communication between people within any form of community can make the difference to whether or not that community remains sustainable.

How we listen to and speak to one another communicates far more than just the words being conveyed in the conversation. It says a great deal about our character and in what sort of regard we hold the other people. Listening attentively and thinking before we speak not only enhances our personal and working relationships, it can be an indication of our maturity, especially our emotional maturity.

From my experience in studying, researching and working with interpersonal communications for several decades, it has become clear to me that a large part of what is being communicated, whether we are speaking or listening to someone, is an intention to influence the feelings of that person. This might be to influence how a person feels about us or to influence how that person feels about him or herself. This is the reason we will seem attentive when we are listening to some people and not with others. These are some of the reasons why we might say kind, caring and supportive things to some people and the opposite to others. Whether we are consciously aware of it or not we will have an intention to influence the thoughts or feelings of everyone with whom we communicate.

For a group or community to work together cooperatively, harmoniously and effectively it would be wise to pay attention to the communication among those involved.

> Having Constructive Communication as an essential element in a community's culture could be very supportive to life within that community and its effectiveness and sustainability.

Listening Constructively

We are listening constructively when we show that our intention is to listen and understand. There are a number of ways we can do this:

a. By stopping what we are doing and giving our undivided attention to the person who is speaking.
b. By allowing enough time to satisfactorily complete our conversation.
c. By choosing suitable settings in which we can hear clearly.
d. By encouraging people to fully express themselves.
e. By listening with compassion and an open heart and mind: without interruption, judgment or criticism.
f. By avoiding the temptation to give advice or fix people's difficulties before those people have had a chance to work things out for themselves.
g. By clarifying anything we don't understand and check out that what we heard was what was actually said or meant.
h. By making sure that people have said everything they need to say and have felt accurately heard and fully understood.

Speaking Constructively

This means speaking respectfully, clearly, directly, honestly, compassionately and supportively. We can do this by:

a. Speaking respectfully to all people at all times.
b. Saying what we mean and meaning what we say.
c. Clearly stating our ideas, suggestions, opinions and conclusions.
d. Honestly expressing how we feel about any situation.
e. Avoiding leaving things out, covering up emotions, pretending all is well or denying what it is we want or need.
f. Giving supportive feedback about what we observe.
g. Speaking kindly and avoiding gossip.
h. Being compassionate by avoiding making judgments and criticisms unless these are constructive and supportive.

If there is very little of this type of communication going on and people in a community speak unkindly, abrasively, disrespectfully or rudely to one another, there is poor communication within that community. Poor communication happens when people listen and speak to each other in ways quite opposite to those listed above. From my research and experience I believe this type of communication to be much more than just poor; I believe it to be destructive.

> Destructive Communication is the opposite of Constructive Communication in every way, as are the results and consequences.

➢ Where Constructive Communication builds trust and mutual high self-esteem – Destructive Communication harms both.
➢ Where Constructive Communication develops relationships and supports cooperation – Destructive Communication undermines both.
➢ Within a community context, Constructive Communication provides a foundation and a framework for effective, harmonious and enjoyable collaboration - whereas, Destructive Communication often creates discord and rips at the heart of good will.

Individuals recognizing tendencies towards Destructive Communication within a community or a community initiative might reconsider being involved. On the other hand, they might prefer to offer to improve the communication aspect of the community culture.

> You can make the difference to your community by eradicating damaging aspects from your own communication and ensuring that your communication with other members of your community comes from the above list of Constructive Communication.

In bringing Constructive Communication into your community culture you may need to do so with compassion and respect. Compassion and respect for those to whom this might be a challenging concept. Compassion and respect for yourself as you endeavor to support this shift. It is crucial to not make anyone out to be wrong, bad or stupid if their ways of listening and speaking are sometimes the opposite of those listed, or if their style of communication could be described as poor or destructive. To be unkindly critical of these people would itself be poor or destructive communication!

It is important to remember that none of us know what we don't know. Constructive Communication might not have been present to any great extent in some people's lives, and so, to those people, many elements of what I describe as destructive communication may seem quite normal and acceptable. Mutually respectful communication might not be a keystone in the families or the culture in which some people live. Many people may not think about how they communicate. They might not associate their way of listening or speaking with some of the difficulties that they experience in their relationships.

Constructive Communication is rarely a priority subject in the school curriculum nor is it often an important subject in most professional training programs. It is my belief that if this were to change then many of our social problems might be eradicated in a couple of generations. Until that happens, we can all do the best we can to make a positive difference to the communications in which we are involved.

Self-disclosure

The period when a community initiative is being established and the times when new people join a community can be used to consciously engage in some trust development. During some of the preliminary meetings, especially during the first one, time could be spent on people introducing themselves to one another in depth and in detail.

An aspect of building trust through communication is that of self-disclosure. This is when people talk openly about themselves, what's going on for them and how they are thinking and feeling. Unfortunately, this can be rare, even frowned upon or discouraged in some places.

> Trust is commonly greater in places where people know a lot about one another; either because of their shared history or because of information learned through their mutual self-disclosure.

To some people, self-disclosure might be okay within families or between close friends. However, it might feel uncomfortable or threatening for them within a group of relative strangers. This can create a Catch-22 situation where people don't feel safe enough to talk about themselves and what they're really thinking or feeling because there is not enough trust in the group or community. And yet, there isn't enough trust in the group or community because people are not being honest and open about their thoughts and feelings.

Obviously, when talking about yourself, your concerns, your ideas, your thoughts and your feelings within a group or community, or anywhere else for that matter, it is important to use 'I statements': 'I notice... I think... I feel... I wonder... I have concerns about... I am alarmed to hear... I feel it might be better if we... I would like... I need to... etc., are suggestions of effective ways to start a sentence of self-disclosure.

> You can make the difference in your project or community by gradually and carefully becoming increasingly self-disclosing.

Self-disclosure can be introduced among group or community members by gently encouraging more of it in informal conversations, community discussions and in meetings. This can be a powerful tool for creating a change in attitude towards speaking openly. I have observed immense relief being experienced by people in communities and local initiatives who realize this gives them permission and opportunity to speak honestly.

If there is a strong culture of people being aloof with one another and keeping themselves to themselves within any form of community then the concept of self-disclosure will need to be introduced with compassion and sensitivity. This could prove to be well worth the effort when openness and honest communication begins to underpin trust.

Eradicating blame

In addition to self-disclosure, attention could be paid to eradicating blaming and shaming language within your community. When people develop the skill of talking about a situation without attempting to shift the blame away from themselves, or apportioning blame to others, the more opportunity there will be for trust to develop.

> The greater the likelihood for trust to grow is when things can be discussed openly, without any attempt to shame or embarrass the people involved.

Giving instructions

Constructive Communication is a firm foundation for the delivery of instructions or directions.

> It is vital that the person delivering instructions knows exactly what these are intended to achieve.

Time is often wasted when the people in charge of a task have not given sufficient thought to how best to give the instructions for it. This is inefficient and wasteful of a community's resources. In a volunteer situation, it also shows disrespect to those who gift their precious spare time for the benefit of the community. For instructions to be fully effective they need to be delivered in a way that those receiving them can easily understand. They are also most effective when given to the people with the appropriate skills and experience who have a sufficient amount of time available to carry them out.

To ensure that the instructions have been heard accurately a useful habit to develop within the culture of the community is that of requiring instructions to be repeated back by the person receiving them to the person delivering them. Whilst this may seem a little contrived, odd or even silly to some people, my experience is that this can save a great deal of time, effort and money. After giving direction or instruction it can prove beneficial to say something like: 'to make sure that I have included everything, please will you repeat back to me what you heard me say?' You can also model this behavior by always repeating back any instructions that have been given to you: 'Let me check that I've got everything...' 'I want to make sure that I haven't missed anything...' 'I heard you say...'

If there is any doubt that some people might not be able to accurately deliver or understand instructions then it could be wise to create instruction sheets for some regular tasks. This could be helpful to newcomers and would be a sensible thing to do if there is a high turnover of volunteers.

Giving verbal feedback

Feedback given to other community or group members might be to appreciate them for what they are doing or to praise or complement them on work well done. Feedback may of course also be to express concern about someone's actions or behavior, to tell them that they have made an error or to explain to them how something needs to be done differently.

It is worth remembering that the trouble is many of us have difficulty in expressing ourselves or delivering feedback in an appropriate way. We might feel awkward, embarrassed or not want to risk upsetting people. So, we might avoid saying anything and so give no feedback at all, in which case nobody learns and a situation is likely to worsen; we may be vague in giving them feedback, in which case people do not understand what we are really trying to convey; or, we deliver the feedback harshly, as criticism or judgment, and in a manner that can be demoralizing and disempowering for the recipient.

On some occasions, harsh feedback or responses might be directly aggressive and made for the benefit of the person delivering them. Often, someone's intention when delivering aggressive kinds of responses is to vent their anger or to relieve their frustration. Or, it might be to seek revenge on that person or to make himself or herself feel better through embarrassing or humiliating that person. On the occasions when no direct response is made or a person is discounted or ignored; that is a passive form of aggression.

It seems to me that there is no need for any of this unkind feedback or response, which I suggest would fit under the heading of Destructive Communication. In my experience, this kind of feedback is rarely beneficial to anyone and often undermines the self-esteem of the person receiving the feedback; damages the relationship between the two people involved and can create problems for the community.

> Clear, honest, direct feedback does not need to be delivered in a critical or judgmental manner. It can easily be delivered with understanding, kindness and compassion. Using 'I' statements encourages people to take responsibility for their feedback.

Supporting improvement

We all make mistakes from time to time. We might not carry out instructions accurately and we don't always behave in the most appropriate manner. The whole point of feedback is to help one another to improve, to develop, to grow.

> We can all change our behavior and learn to do things differently or better.

All we usually need is to be told in a way that we can hear and understand without feeling wrong, bad, stupid, hurt or rejected.

It is important to remember when delivering feedback that even when you are making a great effort to do so supportively, you are likely to be challenging someone's actions, behavior or methods of communication. Hearing this can be uncomfortable for people, especially if they are not used to being challenged. Some people overreact or react very strongly to any form of criticism, real or imagined.

> There is always a supportive way to respond and to deliver feedback constructively, even when people have made errors or their behavior, communication or actions have been inappropriate or have created problems.

Creating a feedback sandwich

Feedback that might be uncomfortable for someone to hear could best be delivered in a 'feedback sandwich'. That is achieved by saying something that might be uncomfortable for someone to hear in between two slices of appreciation, encouragement or praise.

Feedback that is constructive contains a clear statement of the situation, a description of how the person responding or giving the feedback thinks and feels about it and a request or a suggestion for that kind of situation to be handled differently in the future. This can all be easily achieved in what I call a complete message.

Complete Messages

A message is any remark or statement intended to inform people about how we experience any situation.

> A Complete Message makes clear what we observe, think and feel about any situation and what we wish or would prefer to happen next or on similar future occasions.

All relationships thrive on complete messages. People can't know the reality of any situation unless we share all our experience of it. It means giving accurate information about what we observe and clearly stating our thoughts and conclusions about that. It means saying how we feel about it. It means making straightforward requests for what we need or for what we want to happen next. It means requesting different behavior or offering suggestions if we see possibilities for improvement or change.

Leaving any of these out of a message can create confusion and distrust for the following reasons:

1. People could be irritated, offended, antagonized or turned off when they receive judgmental remarks.
2. They are likely to be defensive when they feel they are being criticized or interrogated.
3. They may be suspicious of conclusions people arrive at that are not supported by observations of the reality of the situation.
4. People are likely to be resistant to making a change in their behavior unless they understand the detrimental consequences of that behavior on others.

> People who are defensive, angry, suspicious or turned off, are unlikely to clearly hear responses or feedback or information they are given.

Creating Complete Messages

The idea of a complete message is to deliver information to people about their actions, communication or behavior and your response to those in a holistic way to avoid misunderstandings and hurt. To say things in a way that people will be able hear comfortably and understand what you are saying without becoming defensive, argumentative or aggressive.

Complete messages are best kept simple, informative, honest, direct and spoken in a calm and respectful manner.

 **STEW**

An easy way to remember the elements needed for a complete message to be complete is to make a stew:

1. **S** See: what you notice/observe.
2. **T** Think: what you think about the situation.
3. **E** Emotion: how you feel about it.
4. **W** Want: what it is you wish, want or would like to happen next or in future similar situations.

With practice, you can learn to quickly put together a complete message for every occasion with family, friends, in meetings, and in most situations

It may take a little time to retrain yourself to not react to things that upset you. However, if you can do this, and make the effort to create and deliver your thoughts or feedback to people in a way that they can hear it and learn from it, your relationships could improve, and you are more likely to achieve the results you want.

Delivering Complete Messages

Make your message direct

You know what you really want to say, so say it directly. It's pointless assuming that people know what you think or want. People are poor mind readers; they have no idea what is going on inside you. Save yourself and everybody else time and trouble by being respectfully direct.

Make your message immediate

If you're concerned, hurt, angry or needing to change something, delaying your communication will often increase these feelings. Over time, smoldering irritations can develop into strong resentment, which might then be triggered to explode into rage. Immediate communication can quickly solve difficulties and create or improve trust. Here-and-now communications are more effective and are likely to strengthen relationships.

Make your message clear

Clear statements will be complete and accurate reflections of your observations, thoughts, feelings and needs. Avoid leaving things out, avoid being vague, and avoid being abstract or using jargon. Avoid asking questions when you really need to make a statement.

Make your message congruent

This means ensuring the content of your words, your tone of voice, your facial expression and your body language all say the same thing.

Make your message straight

A straight piece of information, response or feedback is one in which the stated purpose is identical with the real purpose of the communication. Ask yourself a number of questions:

1. What is it I need to say to this person?

2. Why do I need to say it?
3. What do I want him or her to hear?
4. What do I want him or her to do next?
5. How do I wish similar situations to be in the future?
6. How can I best say these for the benefit of us both?

Being straight means being honest, bringing the real agenda into the open and asking for what you want or need to happen.

Use 'I' statements

Saying how you feel about something, rather than making an accusation, is less likely to create defensiveness in the listener.

Saying: 'I feel upset that... I am anxious about... I get concerned when... I wonder what...?' is easier for people to hear than: 'you didn't... You always... You make me...' etc. Wherever possible, avoid the word 'Why?' Using this word can make a message sound like an accusation or an interrogation.

Make your message supportive

It would be wise to adhere to the following guidelines to avoid the risk of people feeling hurt, offended and defensive:

a. Avoid using labels such as: stupid, selfish, mean, disgusting, worthless, lazy, etc.
b. Avoid making accusations such as: 'you're wrong... you do everything badly... you are such a difficult person!'
c. Avoid using sarcasm; it demonstrates contempt.
d. Avoid dragging up past similar situations - to do so might prevent any chance of clarifying how each of you feels about the present situation.
e. Avoid negative comparisons between people: 'you are not as efficient as...'
f. Avoid making judgmental 'you' statements: 'you are... you don't... you never... you always'.
g. Avoid making threats. Making a threat, whether or not you are able or willing to carry it out, is very likely to bring co-operative communication to a screeching halt.

Make your message compassionate

It is unlikely that you will know the full extent of what's going on in anyone else's life. Even people you know well might have issues, concerns, thoughts and feelings that they have not disclosed to you. This is even more likely with people you don't know very well or with whom you have only a slight relationship. There may be reasons about which you know nothing that might be affecting a person's actions and behavior.

It is useful to remember that information or feedback that is given with a sense of compassion is likely to be more effective than if it is delivered without any thought to the recipient's feelings.

At the same time you could have some compassion for yourself. It may take some careful thought, self-control and sometimes courage to make a response, offer feedback or appropriate information intended to bring about the changes or improvement in another person's behavior or actions for the benefit of the community or project.

One flowing statement

It is important to deliver your complete feedback in one flowing statement and without breaks or hesitation.

That way, all of the elements in any message are expressed before the other person makes a response to only just one element. Hearing all these aspects of the situation from your perspective and your experience will give the person a greater understanding of the bigger picture. This can help them to receive this information without feeling the need to be defensive or to react negatively. It could also help to avoid that person experiencing feelings of hurt or disempowerment.

Responding, giving feedback and sharing information in complete messages can help to avoid win/lose, good/bad, wrong/right situations.

Remember the basic guideline regarding constructive communication is to communicate in the way in which you would like to be communicated with.

Constructive Communication is described in detail in three books in this series: SMART TALKING, SMART LISTENING and SMART TALKING & LISTENING TO CHILDREN that are available as paperbacks and e-books from Amazon and accessible through our website: www.youmakethedifference.net

9

ACQUIRING RESOURCES

It might come as a surprise to find the subject of acquiring resources so far into this book.

I know how important resources are and that the objectives of most communities could not be reached without them. However, the acquisition of resources can feel so essential to some communities and community initiatives that people might concentrate their efforts on this issue above all others. This sometimes happens before people are quite clear about what they're attempting to do, how they are going to achieve objectives and how they are going to work, meet, communicate and make decisions together.

My experience is that when the strategies of these are in place people are in a better position to find, create and ask for the resources they need.

> Communities showing clear objectives, workable systems, strong commitment and the evidence of a mutually supportive community culture, stand a better chance of getting their required resources.

Ask for what you need

My great grandmother taught me: 'those who don't ask - don't get!'

And yet, some people have difficulty in asking for what they need. This could be because they fear rejection or simply do not know how to make effective requests.

On the other hand, I have met people who believe that because their project is important then whatever is needed will simply turn up. It seems to me to be passive and even somewhat arrogant to assume this and to imagine that little effort needs to be made to acquire necessary resources. I have heard people described as being good at manifestation. However, I have noticed that most of those people who seem to have the power of manifestation are very clear about what is needed, have strategies for acquiring it and have the ability to make straightforward requests - often accompanied by some power of persuasion.

> Whatever your community needs, ask for it!

In most situations, there will be at least a 50-50 chance for a positive response. If the answer is yes, be grateful, and if the answer is no, then make sure the door is left open for a change of mind. If the odds seem to be less in your favor then do what you can to improve them. Be enthusiastic about the initiative; be clear about its purpose; have details to hand about the objectives, how they will be reached and who will be involved.

Exercise your requesting muscles and practice your asking techniques whenever opportunities arise - making sure that those opportunities are convenient to the people you are approaching. People will not usually mind being asked if they see that a local community is making a difference to the lives of its citizens or an intentional community is doing important work and that the members are committed to it. Many might feel flattered at being approached. However, do this good-naturedly.

Accept any refusal with good grace, with a smile and acknowledgement of people's time and their willingness to listen to your request. Avoid showing disappointment, disillusionment or resentment at refusals that might make it difficult or even impossible for these people to be approached again in the future.

> Avoid seeing a refusal as a rejection of the community, the project, or of yourself.

Stay positive. Have people around you who will support you in staying positive. Look around for other opportunities.

Being skilled in making requests is usually essential for the success of any project; whether that's in asking for occasional help or in requesting major funding. There ought to be at least one person with this capability in any community.

Fundraising

Raising money for community projects can be difficult and may take a lot of time, effort and attention. It's useful to have people in the community who are experienced in finding sources of funding and in creating fundraising events. People with the ability to write successful funding applications are worth their weight in gold.

The following guidelines for filling out a funding application could be useful:

1. Make sure that the project fits the criteria for which the funding is offered.
2. Understand exactly what information the funders require.
3. Know where to place the emphasis in asking for what is needed.
4. Support the application with facts, figures and intended outcomes. These will usually include: the need that will be fulfilled; how and when that will be done; what the outcomes are intended to be; how these will be achieved and how all of this will be measured.
5. Have additional information already formulated in case it is requested.
6. Be certain that your information is correct.
7. Avoid waffling.
8. Write legibly and spell accurately.
9. Keep within the application's guidelines for the number of sheets or the number of words to be used.
10. Check and double-check every detail of the application.
11. Send off the completed application well before the deadline required by the funders. (They may need further information).
12. Have everyone involved hold the vision of the application being successful.
13. Have a letter of acceptance and thanks already prepared for when the application is approved.

Remember: Have all the data used in all applications filed and readily to hand and keep facts and figures updated.

I have observed people attempting to fill in applications without knowing vital facts about their project or where to find this information. Even if one person is responsible for fundraising, others ought to be involved and at least know the answers to rudimentary questions and where to find any facts they don't have, such as who were the biggest funders of the project in the previous 3 years and for how much.

Selection processes

I suspect that in coming years it is going to be increasingly difficult to find funding for some community projects even from traditionally reliable sources. Because of the global financial situation, funding bodies are likely to receive a growing deluge of applications - far greater than the money available. Funders will need to be even more selective than they have been in the past and some of them have already been very selective!

I have witnessed some draconian elimination processes of funding applications. Here is an insight into such selection processes:

Years ago, I attended a workshop on writing successful funding applications that was put on by a major funding agency. I learned that the first part of their selection process was to discard any application that didn't come up to scratch. Poorly written and unclear applications did not make it past this stage. Some applications were not even read beyond the first page. I remember a description, narrated with derision and sarcasm by the workshop leaders, of one application that had been dismissed out of hand when three spelling mistakes were discovered in the first few lines. It seemed to have escaped the funder's notice that this application was for capacity building for people in a project run by a group of immigrant women who were most likely poorly educated and whose first language was probably not English!

It seems probable that when overwhelmed, even conscientious and compassionate funding bodies may be obliged to find reasons to discard many applications at the first stage. Make certain that yours are not among them! To prevent this, every effort will need to be made to make your application as perfect as possible, to stand out from the rest, to attract the funder's attention and to be irresistible to them.

Crowd funding

Crowd funding is not a new concept. For centuries the money for statues and buildings to commemorate significant people or events throughout the world has been raised through some form of crowd funding, although it has only been called this in recent years.

Communities are ideally placed to raise money through crowd funding. Local people, even those not directly involved in community regeneration, might be happy to contribute financially towards improving things, especially if they are likely to benefit. This also applies to intentional communities. The people currently involved; those previously involved; people who have been supported by and those who are in support of the work of an intentional community may be pleased to offer a financial contribution through crowd funding towards projects in the community.

The Findhorn Foundation is an example of this. The Foundation is the original and largest of the thirty or so organizations that now make up the community, although for many years it was the only one. Since the 1960s a significant proportion of the money to buy land, to purchase, build or renovate buildings and to buy vehicles and equipment has been through a variety of forms of crowd funding. The 'crowds' providing the funding are past and present community members, former participants in Foundation workshops and training programs and worldwide supporters and admirers of the Foundation and community.

> Some creative thinking to make crowd-funding initiatives interesting and even exciting could engage a lot of people and help them to feel part of something beneficial to which they can make a difference.

Receiving funding

While there are many difficulties in applying for funding, there can be some pitfalls to receiving it.

The process for getting funding and receiving grants can be a minefield for the unwary. It might be difficult to work out whether or not a community project fits the criteria for specific funding. It can sometimes feel almost impossible to comply with restrictions and achieve the required measurement of outcome while delivering a project with integrity, good humor and without stress.

> In my experience, some types of funding are not worth the effort!

In some circumstances obtaining funding is a bit like getting a mortgage. The mortgage provider actually owns the property until the mortgage is repaid. A community that is totally dependent upon one or a small number of funders might find most of its decisions being influenced or even dictated by the criteria of those funders.

I have observed situations where groups have been obliged to drastically modify their project, its management and the ways of achieving objectives in order to receive or to maintain funding. Occasionally, this has been to the benefit of all concerned, although, often, it has led to group members feeling impotent, frustrated, disillusioned and dispirited. It might be wise to be aware of what you're giving away in order to receive.

> Some funding opportunities may have strings attached that need to be carefully examined. Very occasionally there might be an agenda behind some offers of funding.

Some of the changes taking place within society, such as increased citizen involvement and empowerment are not to everyone's liking. Wise people holding traditional positions of power, nationally and locally, encourage this involvement. Others do not. Sensible people can see the benefits of projects and communities that are alternative or complimentary to those in the establishment. Others might not. On occasion, a community project can achieve great success where similar projects within the establishment seem to be less successful.

It might be wise for people in such circumstance to be circumspect about receiving offers of financial support from some sources. There may be need for vigilance when considering funding for community projects that some people might consider threaten the status quo.

Here is a cautionary tale:

In Canada in the early 1990s a group of parents who had been homeschooling their children got together to create an independent school for their young teenagers. Some of the parents were teachers and those who were not provided whatever other skills and hands-on work and support that the school needed. They remortgaged their homes or borrowed money to buy a property in which to house the school.

Together the children and parents ran the school. The children made the decisions about their education with guidance from parents and teachers. Any child could learn whatever subject he or she was keen to learn, regardless of their age, (none of them avoided any of the necessary basic subjects). If more than six children wanted to study a subject not taught by one of the parents then an appropriate teacher was hired for a few hours each week to cover that subject. For some other subjects the children attended classes in those subjects at local state schools for which they paid the fees.

The children excelled and by the second half of the 1990s several of the pupils under the age of 19 had already attained at least one academic degree.

I discovered the existence of this school when four of the pupils came to the Findhorn Community to attend a weeklong conference on Ecovillage Development. Because the youngsters didn't have enough money to cover the cost of attending, they offered to pay what they could, camp out, and to engage in work exchange.

The arrangement was that two of them, in rotation, would be in the conference sessions, while, which ever two were not, would help to cook, clean and assist with the administration of the conference by doing such things as the photocopying. The youngsters attending sessions made notes on their laptops. The information and results of any activities in which they did not take part were recorded by interviewing those who did. These notes were used in the creation of the Conference Report that was part of their contribution towards the cost of attendance.

These young people seemed to learn more about Ecovillage development than many other attendees of the conference. They took this information home to share with their fellow pupils and no doubt used to good effect in their lives. These young people were confident, bright, efficient and capable. They were interested in everything. They were good communicators and a joy to be around.

I arranged to visit the school when I was in Canada the following year - I was in for a shock!

There I learned that several years previously the Local Authority had informed the school that it was eligible for some financial support to cover the cost of the classes that the youngsters were attending at the local state schools. Over the intervening years this had amounted to a great deal of money. Suddenly, out of the blue, it was revealed that this Authority had discovered an error had been made and that the school was not actually entitled to this financial support.

Any further classes the children attended would once more have to be paid for by them. More seriously, as it was taxpayer's money that had apparently been wrongly allocated, the school was legally obliged to repay every cent.

In spite of great efforts in challenging this decision, it was upheld and a deadline imposed. There was no way that the fundraising options available could raise the amount to be repaid in time. All the parents involved were already stretched to their financial limit, which made further borrowing impossible. With so much stacked against them, including potential litigation, the decision was made by parents and pupils to sell the school property to cover the cost of the required repayment.

After much soul-searching, it was agreed that without the building and because of the levels of stress being experienced by those involved, including the youngsters, it was not possible to continue. The school was closed down.

From this I have learned there may be occasions when it's wise to look a gift horse in the mouth!

Borrowing

Communities – intentional or local - that will be generating funds through their activities may be able to borrow money needed for startup or development.

Although traditional banks are usually reluctant to lend to those organizations that are attempting to deal with escalating social issues, there are some banks that are opening up loan finance to give these organizations the tools with which to help themselves.

One such bank in the UK is Charity Bank, the social savings bank that has supported such organizations across the UK since 2002. It invests all of its money in charities and other organizations whose mission is to improve community or the environment. Details of all investments are published and depositors are not only kept informed, they are encouraged to actively engage with the recipients of Charity Bank loans.

Another UK bank that makes loans available to some charities and community projects is the Co-operative Bank, which is customer-centric and member-led. The Co-operative Bank's Ethical Policy, which has existed since 1992, ensures that it will always stand up for the issues that customers feel passionate about. Customers have a say in what is done with their money and on the issues that matter to them, such as human rights, animal welfare, fair trade and care for the environment. The customer/members also share in profits the bank makes. There are similar banks in many other countries.

More people are beginning to realize that there is an alternative to depositing their savings in the main High Street commercial banks, where they will have no idea what use their money is put to. More of us are moving our money to where we believe it could do some good, such as the banks already mentioned and a few others. This does not only apply to banks. Some of those wanting to have their money used for the benefit of local people are placing their funds in local Credit Unions. An increasing number of people are investing their money in other such regulated institutions as Savings and Loan Organizations and Industrial and Provident Societies.

There are a variety of examples of local and national financial organizations around the world. In New Zealand for example there is Prometheus Finance, a Qualifying Financial Entity (QFE) that was established in 1983 as a Charitable Trust following the example set by a number of social-finance organizations in Europe. Prometheus lends to a range of sectors and activities throughout New Zealand ranging from renewable energy, through sustainable agriculture and energy-efficient housing, to resource recovery and habitat protection.

These and many other types of institutions may be willing to loan to communities and projects that can clearly show that they can fulfill the conditions of the loan.

Community self-financing

There are some ways for intentional communities and community-led regeneration projects to be self-financing to some extent, These can include providing goods and services through a Social Enterprise and initiating a system through which to attract and manage community investment.

In the early years of this century the Findhorn Community was re-formatting itself and building the Ecovillage. There were many necessary projects that required funding and there existed a powerful intention to be as self-sustainable as possible. Working with the support and guidance of the UK Financial Services Authority (FSA), we created Ekopia - our Community Resource Exchange. Formed as an Industrial and Provident Society and Social Enterprise, Ekopia has provided the mechanism for local investment opportunities within the community.

Through Ekopia, finance has been raised for the construction of a Wind Park, the Community cooperative buyout of the local shop and its development into the Phoenix Community Stores, 2 cafes and a bakery. There have been other loans from Ekopia for many more community projects, large and small, including the independent Waldorf Steiner School. Through having this mechanism in place, and with Ekopia as a founding member of Development Trusts, moneys have been made available to the Community for such things as affordable housing.

It has been a joy to see how this local financial initiative has improved economic sustainability and helped the Community to flourish. For information on the varied work and achievements of Ekopia visit: www.ekopia-findhorn.org.

Complementary currencies

There is now a growing movement in some countries towards the creation of local community currencies. These, in complementing national currencies and other forms of barter and exchange, are supporting individuals and communities to become more self-sustaining.

In complementary currency schemes, money is exchanged for notes, vouchers or tokens, usually of equal value to the national currency, which can be spent with any participating individual or business member in the scheme. Usually, each issue has a limited lifetime and the end date is printed on each one. At that time the notes can be redeemed for money to the same value or exchanging for notes in the next issue.

In 2003, through Ekopia, and with further assistance from the FSA, the Findhorn Community created a local complementary currency - The Eko. The community has now enjoyed the benefits of four issues. This has encouraged trading within the Community and with the other individuals and businesses in the local area that wished to participate. These include pubs, cafes, B&Bs, taxi services, trades and professional people. This means that money exchanged for Ekos, that can only be spent locally, remains in the area for the benefit of local people.

> If there is no such currency system within your local community perhaps you and others could start one!

Being creative regarding resources

The fall-out from the banking crisis in 2008 has gravely affected national, regional and local governments. Many of them have needed to reduce their budgets for public health care, education and the variety of forms of social care in which they are engaged. These have been undergoing radical changes. This has seriously impacted the Voluntary and Community sector and is likely to do so for some time to come.

Sensible, proactive and caring people have often stepped into the breach to fulfill some need that is being ignored or inadequately covered by the state. It is apparent that much more of this is going to be required in the foreseeable future.

> It seems clear that a decreasing amount of funding is going to be chased by an increasing number of Voluntary and Community Groups. This is obviously not sustainable. It is clearly time to think outside the box.

So many people have become fixated on money as being the most important of resources and believe that it is what is always necessary to make anything happen. It ain't necessarily so!

Surely, money is a means to an end and that end might be achieved by all manner of means!

People; a community's most important resource

Sometimes there is no need for money for a community to acquire what is needed. People are the most remarkably resourceful species on the planet and we can be exquisitely creative when faced with a challenge and especially the sustainability of something we care about.

Exchange

In many communities and community projects great efforts are made to raise the money to pay for goods and services needed. Do all of those goods and services actually need to be exchanged for money? Some do of course, and yet, perhaps not as many as we might think. Within most communities there may be many things that could be exchanged for other things.

> All over the world an enormous amount of local trading is now being carried out through some kind of exchange or barter. In this way people who are without much money are able to improve some quality of their lives.

To support this there are a variety of exchange mechanisms in operation. These systems allow people to exchange the skills and commodities that they have for the skills and commodities that they need:

a. LETS (Local Exchange Trading Systems): www.gmlets.u-net.com and www.letslinkuk.net.
b. Time Banking: http://www.timebanking.org
c. Green Dollars.
d. Green Pounds.

Regardless of what these systems are called, most operate in a similar fashion. Time, skills, services and commodities of every description are exchanged for something other than money.

> If any of these systems are available in your community, join them. If none exist, then perhaps you or others could start one up.

Even without an organized local system, some people within communities or community groups could perhaps operate a form of regular or irregular exchange amongst themselves. There may be skills within the community or within one group that could be exchanged for something that another group has in surplus. Some groups have easy access to some things that others don't. How can these be exchanged? What skills and time; the hire of rooms, equipment and vehicles could be offered up for exchange?

The number of potentially exchangeable items might only be limited by the imagination.

> Within any group of people there are likely to be a multiplicity of skills and commodities that could be used for exchange. It might be interesting to conduct an exercise within your group or community to discover what is available.

One community group of people with whom I conducted this experiment filled four sheets of Flipchart paper (in small writing) with their ideas.

What about pooling resources? Does every group have to own all of its equipment? How about a number of groups getting together to purchase photocopying machines, minivans and the like? Some communities have created projects to make equipment available to many community groups. Some of these are publicly funded and some are not.

Of course, such pooling and sharing requires that people communicate clearly with one another; make and keep agreements; take responsibility for caring for equipment and be understanding and supportive towards one another.

Hurray! This also provides opportunities to meet other wonderful people, to discover what good things others are doing in a local area and how they are also endeavoring to make a difference.

Skills mapping

Recognizing that the greatest wealth in any community (as in any organization) resides in the skills and experience of its people is likely to expand thinking and encourage creativity.

A useful strategy would be to create some mechanism through which the skills within the community can be easily identified.

I was elected Listener Convener during the years the Findhorn Community was restructuring and expanding itself through the building of the Ecovillage. One of my tasks was to interview and welcome new members. Through this, and by listening to the existing members, I began to get a sense of how many people in the community had a multiplicity of skills of which most people were unaware. Clearly, creating some way for these skills to be made apparent within the community would help those individuals to earn some income and to benefit others who might want to employ people with those skills. However, the task for discovering the skills and abilities of approximately five hundred people seemed daunting.

The following excerpt from FINDHORN COMMUNITY FABLES explains how this was achieved:

The solution proved to be quite a simple one - a telephone directory! It occurred to me that if we created a Community Telephone Directory with one section listing people's home numbers and another listing their professions, trades and skills, people would recognize it as a simple way for them to make known their skills and abilities.

The skills were listed under a variety of headings such as professions, trades, services, the arts, food, health etc. Although a lot of work was involved in categorizing the various headings and entering the information, there was very little of the anticipated need to chase people for their information. By the time the second updated issue was being produced almost everyone in the Community was listed in the directory.

Such was the variety of skills within the Community that most people were listed several times. The multiplicity of the skills on offer and seeing who could do what, made fascinating reading! Many individuals had wonderfully unexpected combinations of skills. We discovered that people skilled in the building trades also offered such things as Tai Chi, crystal bowl meditation and a variety of healing techniques; gardeners had IT skills; voluntary cooks were therapists; accountants and office workers were also skilled artists and craftspeople. There were some rare combinations such as the dear woman who taught pottery also professionally taught people to be opera singers! (Supported by her skilled tuition a number of our young people have developed exquisite voices and have become professional performers.)

It was revealed that around 20% of Community members were skilled in the healing arts, which included therapists and teachers of all disciplines, a variety of body workers and healers as well as counselors, life coaches and spiritual mentors.

As well as the professions and skills within the Community many useful telephone numbers of people and organizations in the surrounding area were included. Doctors, dentists, post offices, cinemas, schools, restaurants etc were listed, as were numbers for many leisure activities, social welfare, transport, and other services. We also listed some local trades people who Community members had found to be reliable. The Directory now runs to twenty tightly packed A4 pages!

This Community Telephone Directory has given newcomers easy access to the services in the area and has made it simple for people to deal for much of what they need with others within the Community. Not only has this been mutually supportive, it encouraged, underpinned and supported the development of The Eko, our local currency.

Status

It could be interesting and useful to consider the topic of status within community. Seeking status seems to be fundamental to being human. It might be beneficial to pay some attention to how status is usually measured and to ways this could be revised within communities.

Traditionally, a person's status in society is measured by the circumstances of their birth, the power or influence they wield, their wealth and the way they accumulate and display it, their education and the way they use it, their fame or notoriety. Many argue that it is in the pursuit of status in these areas that has brought the planet to the precarious state that it is now in.

> Sadly, in most places around the world these days, very little status is gained by being honest, caring, having high human and spiritual values and strong ethics, being virtuous, behaving responsibly, sharing wisdom and experience or living lightly on the planet.

However, some of the communities with which I have been involved have developed a culture in which status is measured in these ways. Surprisingly, very few of them have done this consciously. Instead, it has often evolved out of a desire for equality within the community and quite frequently is as a result of the material impoverishment experienced in the early days of the community's development. In some cases this has brought about a curiously negative attitude towards money and towards people who have it.

It is worth remembering that there are many people born into privilege and/or have acquired some wealth who are highly moral, caring and responsible individuals. Although they may not yet be in the majority, the numbers of these people are growing and they would be assets to any community.

Money is neither good nor evil

Whilst renouncing money and the trappings of a material life may be an essential aspect of joining a spiritual community based on vows of poverty; this attitude is unlikely to result in the sustainability of community living in the modern world.

> Money is innate; a resource like any other that only has the value we place upon it. Treating it as such rather than something to be avoided or craved after would seem to be a more healthy approach.

The communities that have survived their early beginnings of lack of funds and material goods have done so through being very creative and mutually supportive in their acquisitions of the necessities of life. The communities that have thrived and are on track for long-term sustainability have done all of this as well as adopting a healthy attitude towards money; seeing it as a resource – among many, and devoid of any negative judgment about it, or about community members who have more money than others.

10

DIFFICULTIES, FEEDBACK, REFLECTION, REVIEWS

Dealing with difficulties

Things do go wrong from time to time. The trick is to notice when this is happening, investigate what is going wrong and to immediately take action to put things right. Often the cause for things to stop functioning in the way envisioned is lack of funding, although by no means always. Beware of throwing more money at a problem that could better be solved by some careful consideration.

Having awareness

It would be beneficial to any community to have awareness of the difficulties that can arise:

a. Some difficulties within communities may be practical ones such as lack of funding or other resources – including people.

b. Some are due to changes: changes to regulations or a change in needs and requirements.

c. Some difficulties within communities result from the ways in which the members behave towards one another. Conflicts might be inevitably if people have not developed a spirit of cooperation or learned Constructive Communication skills.

d. Cooperation and community cohesion might be threatened if there is a lack of understanding of the stages of the community's development or adequate attention has not been paid to the evolution of the culture of the community, particularly in reference to the behavior of its members.

e. Some difficulties arise from inappropriate leadership or/and unwillingness among community members to take responsibility, both for their roles within the community and for their personal behavior and communication.

f. Some problems escalate when there are no existing strategies for quickly identifying unforeseen difficulties and unexpected situations or insufficient knowledge and experience within the community for handling them.

Ways to handle many of these difficulties might be found by looking to see which essential elements in the community culture are missing or have been ignored and considering how to now introduce these into the community. Having strategies in place for creative thinking and developing ideas will help those in the community to be positively proactive rather than negatively alarmed.

> It could be helpful for the community to have access to experts in the appropriate fields such as conflict resolution, mediation, financial management, management of staff and volunteers, and to one or more experienced facilitators.

Remember: It is a wise community that has strategies in place for when things do go wrong – which they almost certainly will do from time to time.

Feedback on what is or is not working

Feedback is an important source of information.

It enables people in a community to learn firsthand about its effectiveness or otherwise and to discover what is working well and what is not.

Receiving feedback
There are two ways of receiving feedback - directly and indirectly.

Indirect feedback

This is delivered gradually over time when people don't carry out their roles and responsibilities effectively; there is discontent and disharmony within the group or community; people leave and groups or communities fail.

> This kind of feedback is inevitable if issues are ignored in the vain hope of avoiding criticism and conflict or from avoiding facing problems that might be difficult to deal with.

By putting off or avoiding dealing with difficulties; in not setting up simple means for those involved to give direct and regular feedback to management or to one another, people in communities can create the very situations that they are trying to avoid.

The antidote to this is to have regular opportunities for direct feedback built into the culture of the community.

Feedback Questionnaires

A common practice is for the use of questionnaires for review and evaluation and especially as methods for receiving feedback. This written form may be a requirement by those to whom the group is accountable or to be used as a way to follow-up on decisions and actions. It can be useful to have a practice run to trial questionnaires to ensure that they make sense and really will provide the key information required.

Sometimes questionnaires require no signature and so some people might use this anonymity for making criticism or expressing opinions that they do not have to stand behind or explain to anyone. This might be an easy way of receiving information within a community or local initiative. While this is a way to receive information that might not otherwise be forthcoming this seems to be less than desirable in intentional communities and in some local ones also. I think this creates a lost opportunity for people to take responsibility for what they say and for all those involved to hear perspectives that may be similar to or quite different from their own.

Bear in mind that because questionnaires need to be written, reproduced, handed out, collected in, read, recorded and probably filed away, in some circumstances, such as having small numbers of personnel available, they might be more trouble than they are worth.

Complaints

> Many people fear complaints because they think they are indications of failure. And yet, in most cases, complaints are valuable feedback.

155

People who complain are offering very clear feedback about something they are unhappy with. Complaints are opportunities rather than problems; unless they are unheard, ignored or not remedied.

Obviously, it would be better if there is no cause for complaint in the first place and of course there are people for whom complaining is a way of life. In these cases complaints may emerge as grumble or gossip. Even so, there is maturity and wisdom in seeing complaints as opportunities to improve conditions, working practices and offer better service.

Having strategies for hearing about complaints and grievances and dealing with them in a supportive manner can save a lot of time, effort and resources in the long run.

> You could make the difference by helping community members to turn any of their complaints into direct feedback that can be clearly received and appropriately acted upon.

Direct feedback

Direct feedback happens when the people involved in a community or initiative are able to express concerns, talk about progress, of how things are working or not, and what they are thinking and feeling about things directly with one another and with the people who can do something about the relevant situations. Having Constructive Communication as a core element in a community's culture will support this type of feedback.

Prevention is better than cure! Most difficulties might be avoided by having awareness of what could detrimentally affect functioning and the dynamics within the community. A useful strategy to pursue is that of having regular reviews and opportunities for reflection to identify what is working well within the community and what is not.

Reflections and reviews

In all the activities involved in keeping a community moving forward and doing interesting and exciting things, it is easy to forget to ask if the community is moving in the right direction and in a supportive and functional way.

> Having regular times to reflect and to ask 'How are we doing?'
> is an essential safety check.

Opportunities for reflection and review can be held regularly to monitor the progress of community development as well as for individuals, groups, and the community as a whole to review personal work, achievements and satisfaction. Reviews can also provide opportunities for people to acknowledge one another for work well done and for efforts made.

The number of questions in a review will depend upon the circumstances and the number of people present. In a small meeting each person present could answer these questions in one Go-Round. In larger events, these could be considered in small groups.

> As well as a way of evaluating work, progress and interactions, a few minutes at the end of meetings, activities, discussions and decisions to discuss how effective the processes for these were or how they could be improved upon.

Reflection and review upon progress

Regular opportunities for reflection and review on progress, of working practices, systems and procedures will help a community and its groups and projects to remain effective and relevant.

Questions could be asked such as:

a. How on track are we with our intention and objectives? (There is a process for this later in this chapter.)
b. Name some of the achievements that have furthered the aims of the community's purpose.
c. How effective is the process on…?
d. What is the most important achievement since the last review?
e. What has worked well?
f. What has not worked so well?
g. What could be done differently in the future and what new or different steps could be taken?

Reflection and review on objectives, values, ethics and behavior

Reflection and reviews would be useful for assessing in what ways the objectives are being met and how the agreed Values and Ethics are influencing the behavior and working practices of individuals, of the outcomes of activities and upon the community in general.

> When things go wrong in communities it may be because some people have got their wires crossed about the objectives. The values and ethics of some people might be at odds with those stated for the community.

Consider some of the following questions:

1. Are the aims and objectives that people have 'signed up to' being pursued?
2. Does it seem that the community or initiative is veering away from what people believe to be the objectives and towards something that they are not committed to?
3. Are the agreed values and ethics being implemented?
4. Are these still compatible with those of the individuals involved?
5. Has something in the community changed since people felt inspired to become part of it?
6. Has something in people changed since they joined the community or the initiative?

Working together to identify the answers and deal with the responses to these questions could alleviate current problems and save time and effort later down the track.

Reflection and review on interactions and working relationships

In my experience, uncomfortable working relationships, dysfunctional systems, lack of comprehension of how people need to be supported or managed within a community setting, and little understanding of the development of groups and the culture of communities are the main reasons why many communities fail and why some people might leave a community or cease to be involved in further community initiatives.

> One of the challenges of living and working in communities is that they tend to be full of other people!

Communities are often made up of people from very different backgrounds and who have different approaches to life and ways of working from one another. Whatever activity people engage in and whatever community they choose to join they bring their whole selves to it. They bring their personality, their characteristics, their patterns of behavior, the pain of their past and the hopes for their future. This hope for the future may be the very reason why some people join a particular community or initiative.

> Often the common ground shared by all, the concern, the cause, the reason for people to choose to live and/or work in a community, is enough to hold them together and to work out differences or difficulties.

Sometimes, it is not.

If there are relationship problems between people living and/or working in a community it is wise to deal with those problems to prevent them from escalating and rather than risk the loss of valuable people. This will provide all those concerned with opportunities for personal development. Difficulties between people are rarely all one sided, although they may seem that way from each person's perspective! Working to resolve conflict or disharmony as an opportunity for self-exploration can be extremely rewarding.

> Sometimes the people with whom we have the most difficulty turn out to offer us our greatest opportunity for self-awareness and self-improvement.

Choosing not to examine the part we might each play in an uncomfortable relationship could be a lost opportunity to know ourselves better. Believing that everybody else is at fault is likely to be an illusion. Any unresolved situation within a community that people choose to leave might very well reappear in any other community they choose to join.

A reflection and review would be useful for assessing the quality of interactions between people and in what ways these are affecting the life, work and activities in the community.

This review would enquire into:

 a. What is and has been the most enjoyable aspect of our being together?

 b. What has been difficult?

 c. How constructive are communications between us?

 d. What is one thing that needs more attention paying to it while living or working together?

Items for discussion in such a review could be communication, co-operation, mutual support and respect.

Reflection and review on community membership and engagement

If people feel out of place, dissatisfied, unfulfilled or irritated living and/or working in their community then perhaps they haven't found the right fit. They might be a square peg in a round hole, or expectations, theirs or other peoples, may have been too high. It may be because they feel underused and undervalued.

> Even though some of the work in creating or improving community may be tedious, tiring, challenging, occasionally uncomfortable there needs to be some sense of satisfaction and achievement for all those involved.

On the occasions when the community or the initiative does not seem to be working well for some people it might be because some of the following reasons:

- ➤ Their hearts may no longer be in it.
- ➤ They may not be well equipped for facing the challenges of living and/or working in community.
- ➤ They might be square pegs in round holes.
- ➤ They may have unrealistically high expectations of themselves, of others or of the community in general.
- ➤ Some of the people involved might feel that they have not been accepted or that what it is they are offering the community is being undervalued or unappreciated.

It would beneficial to spend some time reflecting upon and reviewing the current membership situation through the perspective of each of these points. Helping people to check out their current experience against what they set out to achieve with their community engagement; with what they wish to offer and what they hoped to receive from it, would be a beneficial thing to do.

Reflection and review on volunteering

Many communities, whether intentional or local, rely, sometimes heavily, upon volunteers, both from within the community and from supporters from outside. Having capable and willing people involved is obviously beneficial in all forms of community; it could be essential to the sustainability and survival of many of them.

> All community engagement ought to be enjoyable, satisfying and fulfilling for people actively involved, especially for those people whose work, effort and time is given voluntarily.

This review could consider questions such as:

a. How well are people fitting in to the community?
b. How committed are people to the development and sustainability of the community?
c. How suitably are they fitted to their roles or tasks?
d. Is any training they require adequate?
e. Are the skills and talents they are offering being appreciated and appropriately used?
f. How well are people being supported in their life and work?
g. What do they need to become even more effective?
h. Are people feeling fulfilled in this community?
i. What do they require or need to happen for them to feel so?

Reflection and review on next steps

Having reflected and reviewed any of these aspects it would be wise to identify the next steps to be taken to deal with or improve any situations and to move the community forward in the most appropriate ways.

Questions:

1. What steps could be taken to move forward with what has been identified?
2. What will you/we do differently from now on?
3. What changes will you/we now make as a result of what we have learned?
4. What contribution will you/we now make towards fulfilling the agreements that have come out of this review?
5. How will we recognize when those changes have been made?

These sorts of questions can bring further clarity and may provide an obvious forward direction. They can assist in reinforcing key elements of a reviewed issue and can encourage commitment to action.

Review processes and many more useful questions for a variety of situations are among the processes described in the books ENJOYABLE AND EFFECTIVE MEETINGS and EFFORTLESS FACILITATION in the YOU MAKE THE DIFFERENCE series available from Amazon and accessible through our website: www.youmakethedifference.net.

The following three review processes can be very beneficial when a community or initiative is experiencing some difficulty.

1. On Track Review

Intentional communities and initiatives can lose momentum and become ineffective when the people living and working within them do not pay enough attention to keeping aligned with the purpose and objectives. When those involved do not recognize or admit to one another that they are off course for achieving the goals and objectives of the community, this might result in loss of support from inside and outside the community or group. The On Track Review is useful for checking these out.

When the current reality has been honestly recognized then work can be done on identifying what the ideal situation might be and how to get from what currently exists to that on track ideal in the most effective and mutually supportive manner.

Applications
This process is useful in a number of situations:
1. If the community seems to be off track.
2. To review progress at the end of the year or some other significant period.
3. In preparation for the Annual General meeting.
4. When a community or group seems to be losing effectiveness.
5. When a community or group is in some kind of difficulty.
6. As a preparation for an application for major funding.
7. When a community is making a significant change such as restructuring its management or governance structures, redefining itself or its form. An example would be when applying for charitable status.

If this process is carried out by a small group of people everyone could work in one group. If a large number of people participate this process can be conducted in a number of common interest or the stakeholder groups.

Outside Facilitation
This could be an event that would benefit from outside facilitation. If that is not possible then have several group members facilitate so that they might also participate at least partially.

On-track Review process

Step 1. Stating the purpose
The purpose and objective of the community or initiative as currently stated are written up on a board or flip chart that is visible to everyone. This could reveal that some people involved are not completely clear about these. In some cases this might show that these have never been clearly defined, in which case some work will obviously need to be done on clarifying the purpose and objective before moving to step 2.

Step 2. Visualization
Working alone, each participant visualizes the best setup they can imagine to fulfill the community's purpose as stated. Visualizing the Ideal Day within the organization or community is an effective process to use for this:

Ideal Day Process
The participants write down everything they would want to happen during an ideal day in the community in order to be on track to achieve its stated purpose and objectives. They are to put in every exquisite detail they can think of in the areas posed by the following questions:

a. What activities would be engaged in?
b. Who would be engaged in them?
c. Where would these activities take place?
d. What facilities, equipment, resources and support would ideally be available for these activities?
e. How would it feel to work in these circumstances?
f. What would be the ideal outcome of these activities?
g. Anything else?

These questions are each addressed as the Ideal Day is described as though it is a diary of the events throughout one day. Starting with the moment of approach the building or first task of the day and ending when there is nothing else to be done on that day.

This process can help to widen thinking. For this reason, I would recommend that in their imaginations, people would consider there to be no restrictions of time or money in the creation of their Ideal Day.

If it can be imagined, it can happen in this Ideal Day.

This is not the time for limited thinking or self-censorship. Some of the more outlandish ideas can be used as metaphors later in the process. If people tell themselves something is silly or not possible, they ought to write it down anyway.

Everything is written about in glowing, positive terms: the sights, sounds and smells, the colors, the atmosphere and the attitudes of the people.

AVK

There are reasons for being aware of the sights, sounds, smells and colors when visualizing an Ideal Day. As was covered earlier we are each usually predominately **Auditory**, **Visual** or **Kinesthetic** in our mode of learning and experiencing. The use of each of the senses while creating the Ideal Day will help to make the visualized activities stronger and more memorable, regardless through which of those modes each person best processes information.

Remembering that the aim is to identify the ideal circumstances through which the community could achieve its goals, each imaginary Ideal Day is to be full, rich, interesting, exciting and joy filled. If it is not like that, it needs to be re-thought.

From experience, I recommend that participants are encouraged to keep writing from the start, regardless of what comes into their minds, rather than spending time pondering or getting their thoughts in some order. A useful trick is to keep the pen point on the paper: this seems to help to keep thoughts flowing.

Step 3. Sharing the day

The groups now reform for everyone to take a turn in reading out their Ideal Day to everyone else in their group. Each Ideal Day description is to be listened to with respect and encouragement. It is important that no derisory remarks or negative comments are made by any of the listeners.

The contents of each person's Ideal Day are indications of the dreams that this person has for the potential of the community. Many of these descriptions will be used as metaphors for what could be made possible.

At the end of each person's story their contribution is to be applauded by everyone in the community with delighted enthusiasm and appreciation. A synopsis of what is said is written up on a board, although no names of who said them are indicated.

Step 4. Finding the common ground

Through a process to identify common ideals by linking similar ideas and grouping related ideals together, a picture will emerge of the ideal circumstances for continuing to carry out the objectives of the community.

Most of the seemingly unrealistic ideas can be seen as metaphors or symbols for changes that could be realized to some extent with some creative thought.

Step 5. What already exists?

Now that people have identified their ideals for achieving the community's purpose it is the time to look at what currently exists.

Working alone once more each person recalls an actual day in the life of the community that they experienced in the recent past. It is useful if the day chosen has some aspects to it that were of concern or that did not turn out so well. To obtain the widest possible snapshot of the life of the community or group, it is important for each person to choose their own specific day, not one dictated by the facilitator.

Everyone writes down all the details of the happenings of their chosen day exactly in the way they experienced it. As with the Ideal Day, this is written down in diary form and every detail is recorded, including the outcomes of any decisions and actions and the feelings that the person experienced. This part of the process is about being realistic, not creative. It is to bring out into the open what already works and what doesn't work so well in fulfilling the community or the project's purpose.

> It is imperative that all information is included. That opinions and thoughts about what works and what does not work well are based upon people's experience.

This is a good way to remember the things to be proud of. This is an opportunity to be realistic about what doesn't work so well in the community, the things to be less proud of.

> Although it is vital for people to be honest, it is not about blaming the system or shaming any individuals.

It is not about bemoaning the lack of funding or railing against an unjust world. It is about identifying and recording the details of what actually happens day to day. To prevent it from becoming a depressing or chastening exercise, the facilitator manages this in a light manner: perhaps lightening the mood by bringing gentle humor in where appropriate.

Step 6. Sharing the reality

As before, everyone then shares with one another what she or he has written down. This is a vital part of the process in that it allows everyone to hear and acknowledge what really goes on from personal experience rather than from the perspective of gossip or rumor.

It might be uncomfortable for some people to speak about or to hear things that might be considered negative. Even so, it is vital to do so. If the pitfalls in previous thinking, current initiatives or ideas for potential projects are not identified then whatever problems or dysfunctional systems or behavior already exist in the community are likely to be perpetuated. This is the ideal time and process for the recognition of those potential pitfalls to come to light.

As before, a synopsis is written on a board. Common themes will probably appear as the areas of related experiences are linked.

Step 7. Getting from here to there

By now, how close to or how far from being on track for the community achieving the highest ideal objectives will have become clear. Perhaps the gap is encouragingly small. Maybe it is alarmingly wide! Either way, the areas that require work will have become apparent.

It is time to consider how to get from where the community currently is, to where it now clearly and ideally would wish to be. Appropriate questions to ask would be:

1. How on track are we?
2. Which parts of the shared ideal are already in place?
3. What parts of the current reality need to be improved?
4. Ought any of these to be discarded altogether?
5. How to fill in the remaining gaps?
6. What new and revolutionary ideas identified in the ideals can be initiated to move us forward to a new and more ideal way of being on track?
7. How can we do that simply and mutually supportively?

This is the time for participants to inspire and empower each other.

Step 8. Working groups

After identifying these ideas, working groups can now be set up to pursue them. If this is a full day event then this work, or at least some of it, could be carried out immediately; otherwise future meetings will need to be set up. A careful record ought to be kept of who will do what and by when and how these will be reported back to all those who have participated in this event.

> Note: To prevent feelings of exclusion and any potential for undermining or sabotaging the outcomes it is important that everyone involved in the process so far is included or suitably represented in these ongoing discussions and decisions.

Ending process

A suitable ending process such as a Go-Round will allow participants to share their thoughts and feelings about the event with everyone in the community or in their new working groups. If time is short then a Paired Sharing will give them the opportunity to share these with one other person.

Closure

The facilitator sums up the process, reiterates the decisions taken, clarifies the work to be done in the working groups and announces the date of the next follow-on meeting at which the working groups will report progress.

Appreciations all round. Close.

2. Mutual Support Group Review

This allows small groups of people to be supportive to one another in their community life and for developing and achieving their visions and goals. Mutual Support is offered within a group setting where people are given the space to think out loud on some current aspects of how their community life fits into their visions and long-term goals.

All the benefits of putting aside time to think; equal opportunities to speak and interruption-free listening are essential in a Mutual Support Group.

Each Mutual Support Group usually numbers between 3 and 6 people. Using Go-Rounds and Think and Listen processes each member of the group in turn answers out loud the following four questions:

Q

1. What is going well for me in this community or initiative?
2. What is difficult for me in this community or initiative?
3. How do these affect my goals and visions for this community or initiative?
4. As a member of this community (or community group) what are my next achievable steps in resolving these difficulties and so move towards my visions and goals?

Each question is addressed for a couple of minutes and a time-keeper is appointed among the group to ensure everyone has an equal opportunity to speak uninterrupted. If support with anyone's identified next steps is needed, this could be offered by other group members or sought elsewhere.

3. Spring Cleaning Review

Sometimes a community is so busy getting on with the work, coping with all sorts of challenges and difficulties such as insufficient funding or lack of workers and helpers, that not enough time, if any, is devoted to morale or dealing with the small things that irritate or upset people and make work or relationships within the community difficult.

This can create problems, because, to use a couple of clichés: most people tend **not** to suffer in silence, and, misery loves company. Gripes and complaints can become the basis for a ground swell of discontent and negative thinking. This can undermine the quality of life in any community; turn working relationships sour and create an atmosphere that nobody wants to live in.

> Attitudes within a community can become tarnished by unresolved small concerns and niggling complaints. It can be useful to devote a review meeting to giving these an airing and finding solutions to them.

The Spring Cleaning method is effective for this as it begins with a Brainstorming session to bring problems out into the open. Although Brainstorming is usually seen as a way of generating positive ideas; it can also be a useful way to get out into the open all the things that are not working well or those that people in a community feel unhappy about. Because it's not always easy to recognize who is saying what in a Brainstorming session, it allows a certain amount of anonymity and safety for people to say the things they may not feel able to openly express in other circumstances.

When all the issues, large or small, have been identified then discussions are held to find solutions to these and to implement systems to prevent or reduce the likelihood of them reoccurring.

I have named this process Spring Cleaning because of its potential result and because it is an effective way of starting a new year in the life of a community, whether this is the calendar year or following after an AGM or the annual community birthday celebration.

> This Spring Cleaning process is metaphorically throwing open the doors and windows of the daily workings of the community, sweeping out the dust of accumulated grumbles, putting the shine back on individual and community attitudes and freshening up the air of mutual support and cooperation.

Details for the facilitation of Mutual Support Group and Spring Cleaning Reviews and many other reviews and processes are in the chapter on Ready Made Meeting Designs in EFFORTLESS FACILITATION, which is available from Amazon and through our website: www.youmakethedifference.net

11

PARTINGS, ENDINGS & COMPLETIONS

Partings

An important aspect of sustainability in any community or project is for those who are leaving to do so responsibly. To give plenty of notice whenever possible to ensure continuity; to prevent progress from being detrimentally affected; and to avoid letting people down.

A final review process can ensure that a person's work has been handed over successfully and that all loose ends have been tied off. It will also provide an opportunity for them to be appreciated for their dedication and contribution to the community or the project.

People choosing to leave

People choose to leave communities and step out of involvement in projects for all sorts of reasons. These may be due to changes to their lives or because they no longer want to be involved.

Occasionally, people leave because they are unhappy with something or someone within the community or group. Their decision to cease their involvement ought not to come as a surprise. Previous conversations, feedback sessions, Mutual Support Groups, reviews and various methods of clear communication ought to have provided ample opportunities to bring whatever the difficulty is out into the open for discussion and remedial action or improvement where appropriate. If these systems do not exist in your community it could be wise to create them.

If self-disclosure or opportunities for regular feedback are not usual within the culture of the community it may not be known why a person is ending their involvement. Some people may of course say that they're leaving for personal reasons when they are not.

It may take courage for them to be honest about leaving because of something that has been upsetting them, especially if they have kept it to themselves or have denied there has been anything they have been unhappy about.

A respectful and supportive Completion Clearing conversation with these people can reveal their reasons and give them an opportunity to give feedback on what has or has not worked for them during their involvement. This type of conversation is not always comfortable for either person and it may take courage and compassion from all concerned. Even at this late stage it may not be too late for a change of mind.

It would be useful to remember that people can be more willing to offer feedback on some issues when they are about to leave than they may have felt able to convey while still fully involved.

It can be helpful to the ongoing development of your group or community for anyone who is leaving in whatever the circumstances to give feedback on such things as their experience of the effectiveness of the management structure, leadership and meeting methods. There could also be wider issues such as living or working conditions, the quality of mutual support and the interpersonal communications.

Such a conversation can clear the air and provide useful information that can be used to make improvements. It might be the last chance to know how a person thinks and feels about the community or initiative and to discover some potentially valuable insights from their perspective.

Requesting people to leave

Communities are made up from all types of people who have a variety of intentions, needs, expectations and patterns of behavior. Not everyone who wants to engage in a group or a community has the skills to get on well with others. Some people can be uncomfortable to be around. Even so, it can be well worthwhile and beneficial to all concerned for such people to have the opportunity to be involved.

However, in extreme circumstances it might become apparent that the behavior and/or attitude of some individuals are not compatible with those of the majority of people involved or with the common ground agreements that have been made. With the best will in the world, it is not always possible to support people to behave in a manner appropriate for community living, or to help them to improve their attitudes sufficiently for them to remain in an intentional community or an active member of a community group. In very extreme situations regarding safety and security in the community it might not be wise for them to do so.

> Any decision to ask someone to leave ought to be arrived at through a transparent community process that includes the individual in question for most or preferably all of the process.

The reason why it is necessary for the person to leave the group or community ought to be clearly and honestly communicated to them. This can be done with kindness, even if a person has behaved inappropriately or in some way reprehensibly. By using the principles of creating and delivering a Complete Message, it will be possible to make the situation clear to this person without humiliating them.

A Completion Clearing conversation could provide an opportunity for things to be said that need to be said. This type of conversation might not be comfortable for those involved and may take a lot of courage and compassion.

Completion Clearings

These conversations can allow people to end their involvement in a community with some grace and leave it with a sense of completion for themselves and the others involved.

> This is not intended to be a last opportunity for a slanging match or for throwing around accusations and unkind criticism.

Remember, completion clearings are always to be conducted in 'I statements'.

Begin by offering some appreciation of the person who is being requested to leave or is leaving because they are unhappy with their involvement. Say something about the positive things this person has contributed. There are bound to be some things to appreciate and it would be helpful for them to leave knowing what those are. Make this appreciation specific and detailed. Not only will this let the person know exactly what you have valued, it could encourage them to be equally specific and detailed when giving their feedback on their experience of the group or community.

Continue by asking if they would like to discuss their reasons for leaving, which could provide an opportunity for the person to bring their experience or concerns into the open. It could help this person to talk about the situation, support them to get over it, and for the group or community to receive information that might prevent a similar distressing situation from occurring.

What is heard from them might be surprising. There may have been things going on about which most people knew nothing. This could provide an opportunity for further conversation with all those involved.

Then offer the person feedback on your experience and/or that of others regarding their involvement in the group or community. This feedback is given using Constructive Communication and is not to be used as an opportunity for unkind judgment or criticism.

There might be things that need to be remedied or apologized for, either by the person leaving or from others, especially if some new perspectives have emerged.

Even at the last minute, a clearing conversation might help a person to change their mind about leaving. Or there may be nothing that could have been done to make the situation any more acceptable to that person. Sometimes it may become clear that they themselves have contributed to the difficult situation or even been the cause of it.

At the end, say one more positive or appreciative thing about the person who is leaving. That concludes the completion clearing.

Completion Appreciation

When someone is leaving who has lived in an intentional community or has played a role in an initiative, a Completion Appreciation process will give everyone who has been involved with that person the opportunity to show their appreciation and offer good wishes. This event might take place on the day of the person's leaving or very close to it. An open invitation could be made to include anyone who would care to attend.

These events are sometimes managed by a facilitator or some kind of master of ceremonies and could be expected to take around an hour, perhaps a little longer if the group is a large one or if the person has been involved with many people over a long time.

Everyone is seated in a circle so that they can see everyone else. The facilitator asks the person leaving to start the process by speaking about their time in the community. This can include what their involvement has meant to them, such things as the highs and lows, and an appreciation of the value of the community or project and of the other people involved.

It is now the turn of those other people to speak appreciatively about that person and their experience of them. In my experience, this appreciation often includes some short anecdotes that may be touching and/or humorous, which all those present can enjoy. Not everyone will need or perhaps want to say something. However, enough time ought to be allowed for most of the people present to speak for a minute or two.

When the facilitator has ascertained that no one else wishes to speak, he or she rounds up the proceedings by also saying something appreciative. The person leaving might like to be given the opportunity for a brief response to what they have heard.

If the completion process is not something that is part of the culture of your community you can make the difference to the way people leave it by introducing this process.

> Whenever possible it is important that people end their involvement feeling that their time has been well spent; that they have gained a great deal from the experience; that they have been appreciated for their efforts and that they have made a difference to the community.

Celebrate

> Whenever possible mark the leaving of people with a celebration.

Have a goodbye party; encourage everyone in the person's group to go out for lunch or, at the very least, arrange for a special cake to arrive during that person's last day. Have a card for people to sign, which could include everyone who has been involved in the person's activities and anyone who has benefited from their efforts. A thank you gift from the whole group or community might be appropriate too. Individuals may want to make their own personal offerings. Whilst flowers and wine are nice to receive, they don't last very long. Offering a gift that has been carefully chosen to be appropriate and significant to that person could be more meaningful and provide them with a long-lasting memory.

Keep the door open

You could make the difference to the people who are leaving by letting them know that they would be welcome back at any time. Whether that's just popping in to say hello to offer occasional volunteer support or to return as a fully committed member.

> Knowing the door is always open to them can reinforce to people that they have made a difference to the community's sustainability and that they could do so again anytime they choose.

Endings

The topics covered in this book will go a very long way towards creating and sustaining successful intentional communities and local community initiatives. Even so, the saying: "all good things come to an end", is sometimes the case in even the most worthwhile and successful projects.

I believe there is a myth regarding sustainability. For some people, sustainability has come to mean ensuring the continued existence of something at all costs, regardless of the quality of that existence or of its remaining relevance. It seems to me that there are some situations when the time, effort and resources required to sustain a project far outweigh the benefits that the project offers. Occasionally, situations will occur, sometimes quite unexpectedly, which make it impossible or perhaps unnecessary for a community project, or even an intentional community to continue. These might come to an end for all sorts of reasons:

a. The reasons for coming into being may no longer exist.

b. There might be a lack of resources. There may come a time when a project ceases to attract the funding essential to be able to function effectively or to continue at all.

c. A significant majority of people involved might move away, experience a change of circumstances or even a change of heart or mind.

d. People can lose energy or interest, especially if there seems to be a continuous uphill struggle. Even the most dedicated people can grow weary.

e. An intentional community or local community initiative that no longer has relevance, especially to the majority of the people involved, is likely to become increasingly difficult and frustrating to work in and sustain.

f. Projects can lose momentum, may become ineffective or lose support because the people in them have not recognized or admitted to themselves that they have already achieved their purpose or that circumstances have changed and they are no longer necessary or relevant in their current form.

Relevance Review

Through participating in a relevance review, people in a community or initiative can evaluate its current and future relevance. Through this it might become recognized that the project has completed its purpose, aims and objectives.

After stating the purpose and objectives of the community or initiative, the incisive question to ask would be:

If this community/initiative did not exist, would we want or need to invent it; if so for what exact purpose and why?

This is a time for courage and honesty. It might not be easy for those involved to recognize that their community or initiative may no longer have real relevance as it currently exists, or that it may need to be rethought or restructured to have continued relevance.

> The most valuable people in the community at this time could be the ones willing to speak the uncomfortable truths.

Responding to 'Yes'

If the majority of people involved feel that the answer to the above question of relevance is 'yes', then the community or initiative may choose to go through the steps of visualizing the ideal set up, identifying the current reality and working out how to bridge the gap between the two in order to become even more effective, productive and relevant in the future. The Ideal Day process described earlier could be useful for this.

Responding to 'No'

If the answer is 'no' then people could spend the rest of the event considering how best to proceed.

Some suggested options:
   a. People consider other ways for them to live and/or work together.
   b. Seek another community initiative to which their skills and resources could be dedicated.
   c. Initiate an Action Search process to identify one or more community projects or initiatives in which to become involved. (This process is one of the readymade meeting designs described in EFFORTLESS FACILITATION in this series.)
   d. Begin steps to wind up the community or the project.

This relevance process may not be easy to conduct if disharmony in the initiative or community is common or if the leader or some people within the community want to retain control. If people are desperate to hang on to their roles or to the very existence of the project, regardless of its ineffectiveness or irrelevance or even having successfully completed its purpose, then this process may be impossible to initiate. This could be unfortunate because these are the very situations where this process is most likely to be needed.

An inspiring outcome from a Relevance Review:

A voluntary community group had for some time been doing excellent pioneering work on recycling in their local area. As their work proved to be successful and public opinion towards recycling improved, the Local Authority created a comprehensive recycling collection system, which effectively made much of the group's recycling work redundant.

Instead of rejoicing in their victory of achieving widespread recycling in their area, the people in the project hung on to their need for existence. In their reluctance to admit to their current situation and apparent irrelevance people spent time criticizing the way the local authority was managing the recycling.

A Relevance Review helped them to see that their original purpose had been successfully completed. This then left them free to make new choices.

They decided to reorganize the project to become more specialized. Some people chose to research the recycling of difficult items such as batteries and used engine oil. Some looked for ways to encourage people to purchase items that had been repaired or recycled and others were interested in promoting approaches to saving energy and resources. These were ideal projects for a volunteer group to engage in, especially in times of financial constraints when there was little money available to pay people to do this kind of work. The group discovered that in its new way of working it had become more relevant than ever.

Leadership: Stepping up or stepping down

At this stage it might be the time for the overall leader to step up to their responsibility of holding the group or community together as it shakes itself into the best new format and with the most suitable systems and methods for achieving its purpose. It may take strength and courage to stay in a leadership role at this time.

On the other hand, this might be the time for a leader to step down. Perhaps the person currently leading the initiative or who has led the community from the beginning might no longer be the most appropriate leader. Maybe the group or community now needs a leader with a different set of skills and abilities.

> The qualities of leadership that it takes to get any project off the ground might not be the ones needed to sustain it; to change it; or to maintain harmony and cohesiveness through those changes.

It could be that the leader has been inspiring the group or community and holding it together until the next appropriate leader could emerge.

> The wise leader knows when it is time for someone else to take on the leadership role. In this case it may take strength and courage to step down.

Winding up

If, after all options for continuing have been explored, the decision is taken to wind up the group or community, it is important that this is done with care and awareness. There are some practical things that need to be addressed regarding assets and commitments when something like this is coming to an end.

Remaining assets will need to be appropriately distributed or disposed of. Any that have been acquired through public funding or other forms of fundraising will need to be offered to another appropriate group or project. All this must be fully documented.

If those in the current project feel unable to continue, and there is still a need for some of the service to others that it has been providing, perhaps there is another group or project that could take over some of that work? Would that be the appropriate group to make best use of any remaining assets? Might those in the group who would like to continue to be supportive to this cause find a place in this other group to which they could offer their experience?

Dealing with the feelings

> During the final stages it is important that all those involved in the community or project continue to be supportive to one another.

Obviously, any decision to close down or wind up an intentional community or a community initiative will not have been taken lightly and all of those involved would have been fully engaged in the discussion, the consideration of all the options and in the final decision.

It is essential for there to be ample opportunities for everyone involved to honestly express their feelings during these discussions. It is likely that some, perhaps all, the people involved will feel disappointed and distressed in the decision to close down.

It can be difficult and painful to wind up a community, especially when it is people's home and particularly if they have lived there for some time. Feelings will need to be acknowledged and some process to allow those feelings to be expressed could help people to recover from their distress and move on with their lives.

Closing down any community project might bring with it a sense of failure or embarrassment, particularly if it has had a high profile. There may be feelings of resentment towards those people, inside or outside of the community, whose actions may be perceived to have been the cause of the closure. Even those people who believe, as I do, that there is no such thing as failure – only opportunities through which to learn – might find that it requires a great deal of strength to keep an open heart towards some people in these circumstances.

It is important to have a review process through which to reflect upon achievements and to recognize successes.

> It could be enormously beneficial to have a completion process to provide those involved with an opportunity to acknowledge one another's effort and commitment; and to offer appreciation for work well done and especially for attitudes of care and support.

Celebrate

At the end of any project it is important for there to be an attitude of celebration of successes achieved and appreciation of all who have been involved.

The more successful a project has been the more cause there would seem for celebration. However, even when a community project has been less effective than intended or has been closed prematurely, for whatever reason, there will still be things to celebrate.

There are certain to be positive outcomes of the project that can be celebrated:

➤ The work that has been effective.
➤ Those occasions when everything ran smoothly.
➤ The coming together of the people in the community.

> ➢ All the things that have been learned.
> ➢ The opportunities for fun, inspiration and the personal development of those involved.

Mark the end with whatever type of celebration feels appropriate.

Options:
  a. A goodbye party.
  b. A potluck supper.
  c. At the very least, arrange for a special cake.
  d. Cards and small gifts might be exchanged among those involved.

Engaging in a comprehensive completion and celebration can help keep the door open to opportunities for people involved to engage with one another in future projects.

Remember, out of this ending, there may come new beginnings. There is plenty of community building work that needs to be done out there!

In Conclusion

There are now a great many examples of fledgling or successful communities and community-led regeneration projects in many parts of the world. This grassroots movement is expanding enormously. I heard it recently described as potentially the greatest social revolution that humanity has seen.

> It seems to me that it is not so much a revolution as more of an obvious and inevitable step in human social evolution!

It appears clear that increased community engagement and more management of society at the local level is the next obvious evolutionary step in humanity's ways of coexistence. As with all forms of evolution this starts with tiny changes that are improvements on what was there before, have been passed on and become integrated. The difference between this human evolutionary step and all previous ones is that this one is being made very consciously.

As with all evolutionary steps, the timing of this one is perfect. Just as we human beings are waking up to our potential for creating a sustainable future together at a local and community level, we have all the technology we need to share information and offer support to one another. Globally there is a wealth of ideas and experiences easily available on what could be done to create vibrant, enjoyable and sustainable communities. The YOU MAKE THE DIFFERENCE series of books and the Free Guides on our website are our small contribution to this. There is much more that can be discovered.

All that is required for any individual to become part of this natural, crucial and inevitable evolution is to make the choice to become part of the solution rather than be part of the problems in their communities; to be willing to explore and engage in some community improvement opportunities, to offer a small amount of time, skill or experience to making a positive difference to their community and to the lives of the people around them. This can be interesting, exciting and empowering, as well as a lot of fun!

MORE YOU MAKE THE DIFFERENCE BOOKS

Ripples created by our actions inevitably make some difference in the world. These books are intended to encourage and help people who want to make a positive difference to their lives and to the world around them.

YOU MAKE THE DIFFERENCE
through
ENJOYABLE & EFFECTIVE MEETINGS

Following the guidelines for constructive participation, for efficient chairing and supportive facilitation, adopting the suggested attitudes, implementing the methods, skills, tools, essential procedures and useful processes will guarantee improved effectiveness and enjoyment of any meeting.

YOU MAKE THE DIFFERENCE
Through
EFFORTLESS FACILITATION

This book is packed with suggestions for planning and designing meetings and events, useful methods and tips for facilitation, empowering and productive processes and a variety of ready-made meeting designs to fit many situations. The implementation of these will guarantee inexperienced facilitators becoming skillful and experienced facilitators becoming even more accomplished – effortlessly!

YOU MAKE THE DIFFERENCE
Through
ENJOYABLE & VALUABLE VOLUNTEERING

Ripples created by our actions inevitably make some difference in the world. This book is intended to help people who want to make a positive difference through their volunteering. It contains simple and exciting methods for people to explore what skills and experience they could volunteer, where and how they can easily make their valuable contribution, how to look after themselves while effectively helping others and the many enjoyable ways in which volunteering will enrich their own lives.

YOU MAKE THE DIFFERENCE
Through
EMPOWERING VOLUNTEER MANAGEMENT

This book contains many suggestions for finding, recruiting, supporting, empowering, managing and keeping volunteers. Following these guidelines and using the insights into what volunteers need to be efficient, effective, valuable and fulfilled in their roles, will guarantee empowered volunteers.

YOU MAKE THE DIFFERENCE
Through
SUCCESSFUL GROUPS & PROJECTS

This book offers insights into how groups work and why they sometimes fail, successful start-up and maintenance of projects that achieve the purpose and objectives, methods for attracting and keeping appropriate members and volunteers. The adoption and implementation of the suggested attitudes, the strategies for obtaining resources, the efficient use of time, money, skills and effort, and the respectful, cooperative ways people can enjoy working together will guarantee success of any group or project.

YOU MAKE THE DIFFERENCE
Through
SMART TALKING

Each time we open our mouths to speak we will inevitably have an impact upon those to whom we are talking. This book aims to show the consequences of having a negative impact and offers insightful suggestions for creating a positive effect. Following these guidelines and the suggested attitudes, skills and tools that can relieve stress, enhance relationships and improve communication in so many areas of life will guarantee anyone becoming a Smart Talker.

YOU MAKE THE DIFFERENCE
Through
SMART LISTENING

Each of us will inevitably have an impact upon the individuals to whom we listen that is either positive and beneficial or negative and potentially damaging to individuals and society. Implementing the attitudes, listening skills, tools and techniques suggested in this book will guarantee a positive effect that will greatly improve personal and working relationships, reduce conflict, enhance many areas of life and be supportive to people's confidence and self-esteem.

YOU MAKE THE DIFFERENCE
Through
SMART TALKING
& LISTENING TO CHILDREN

From the moment children are born they are learning to become the adults who will manage the future. What kind of future might adults be influencing through the way they talk and listen to children? This book is crammed with skills, tools, insights and suggestions on how adults can be supportive through their communication to the development of youngsters and contribute towards a safe, sustainable future in the hands of well adjusted, capable, empowered, responsible and caring people.

ABOUT
YOU MAKE THE DIFFERENCE

Tim and Kay Kay, the two generations of cultural creatives who founded YOU MAKE THE DIFFERENCE, believe that it is now essential for people to behave supportively with another, to become more engaged in their local community and to cooperate and work together for a sustainable future. The books and website are intended to encourage and support people to achieve the positive difference they wish to make in their lives and in the world around them.

To help with this, Kay Kay, the author, offers decades of experience gained in a variety of professions and cultures, and shares her practical philosophy, knowledge, skills and insights into beneficial ways of behaving, working and communicating with one another and contributing to society.

Tim, as collaborator, book designer, publisher and Webmaster, brings his creativity as an artist and writer, his in-depth knowledge of Buddhist philosophy and the skills and considerable experience gained through living, working and studying in many countries.

All the YOU MAKE THE DIFFERENCE books are intended to be enjoyable to read and easy to use - by everyone. The wealth of information is concisely written to be of benefit to professionals wishing to upgrade their skills; busy people working to make a difference in their communities and at the grassroots of their societies, and people from different cultures, especially those from the developing world, for whom English may be a 2nd or even 3rd language.

On the website: www.youmakethedifference.net there is more background information; GUIDES on a variety of interesting and useful subjects that are FREE to download and the opportunity for people to become part of the Global YOU MAKE THE DIFFERENCE network.

"We each make a difference in the world every moment through our words, actions and behavior, whether we are aware of it or not. The trick to being a smart human being is to choose to make a positive difference."

Kay Kay